CHOLESTEROL-FREE

CAKES

& COOKIES

CHOLESTEROL-FREE

CAKES

& COOKIES

ALL-TIME FAVORITE RECIPES ADAPTED

FOR A LOW-CHOLESTEROL DIET

MABEL CAVAIANI, R.D.

AN OWL BOOK
HENRY HOLT AND COMPANY
NEW YORK

Published by Henry Holt and Company, Inc.,
115 West 18th Street, New York, New York 10011.
Published in Canada by Fitzhenry & Whiteside Limited,
91 Granton Drive, Richmond Hill, Ontario L4B 2N5.

Library of Congress Cataloging-in-Publication Data
Cavaiani, Mabel.
Cholesterol-free cakes & cookies : all-time favorite recipes
adapted for a low-cholesterol diet / Mabel Cavaiani. — 1st ed.
          p.   cm.
        "An Owl book."
        Includes index.
1. Low-cholesterol diet — Recipes.   2. Cake.   3. Cookies.
        I. Title.
        RM237.75.C379   1992
641.5'638 — dc20   92-8664
                                                        CIP

ISBN 0-8050-1739-9

Henry Holt books are available at special discounts
for bulk purchases for sales promotions, premiums,
fund-raising, or educational use. Special editions
or book excerpts can also be created to specification.

For details contact: Special Sales Director,
Henry Holt and Company, Inc., 115 West 18th Street,
New York, New York 10011.

First Edition — 1992

Designed by Katy Riegel

Printed in the United States of America
Recognizing the importance of preserving the
written word, Henry Holt and Company, Inc.,
by policy, prints all of its first editions
on acid-free paper. ∞

1   3   5   7   9   10   8   6   4   2

In loving memory of my husband, Charles "Chuck" Cavaiani, for whose sake I started collecting and developing low-cholesterol recipes. His love and support were my strength and joy during the years we shared.

CONTENTS

CONTENTS

COOKIES

ACKNOWLEDGMENTS

I WOULD LIKE to thank the following people for their encouragement and professional help in developing and writing this book:

Mabel Frances Gunsallus, M.S., R.D., of Miami, Florida, who has served as a sounding board for my ideas and whose advice and support have contributed greatly to this and other books I have written.

Mary Boineau, of Tampa, Florida. We have spent many happy and rewarding hours discussing recipes and culinary techniques.

Frances Nielsen of Oak Lawn, Illinois, who has taught me so much about food and food preparation.

My sister Shirley Sniffin of Wadena, Iowa, who tasted, tested, and evaluated most of the recipes in this book.

Edith Robinson, M.S., R.D., of Decatur, Georgia, whose encouragement and wealth of knowledge about low-cholesterol diets has helped me ever since my first cookbook was written.

Patti Dillon, M.S., Fayette County, Iowa, Extension Home Economist, whose encouragement and professional information helped make this book a reality.

Kathy Steege, manager, and Judy Mohlis, assistant, Fayette County

ACKNOWLEDGMENTS

Extension Office, whose capable computerized nutritive analysis of the recipes in this book furnished vital information for those who use it.

Muriel Urbashich, R.D., of Hometown, Illinois, with whom I have written several large-quantity cookbooks. Her support and professional information have always been important to me.

I would also like to express my sincere appreciation for the resources of the following organizations: the American Dietetic Association, the American Heart Association, the Iowa State University Extension Service, the U.S. Department of Agriculture, and the U.S. Food and Drug Administration.

FOREWORD

I'M HAPPY TO KNOW that my friend Mabel Cavaiani has written another interesting and helpful cookbook. I am convinced, as she is, that a diet that includes foods people are accustomed to eating has a better chance for success. The difficulty in adjusting to unfamiliar foods is aggravated when everyone else in the family is eating comforting, familiar foods.

In fact, if someone in the family has a dangerously high cholesterol count, it is a good idea for all family members to follow a low-cholesterol diet, since studies indicate that children whose families have a history of cardiovascular problems and heart disease should be encouraged at an early age to develop proper living habits and diet to maintain normal serum cholesterol levels.

Too many Americans are dying from heart attacks or strokes. This could be prevented in many cases by changing the controllable risk factors, such as diet, exercise, obesity, and smoking. A healthy low-fat, low-sugar diet with increased fiber can help increase the good cholesterol (HDL, or high-density lipoprotein) and decrease the bad cholesterol (LDL, or low-density lipoprotein). It is important to keep the blood cholesterol below 200 mg/dl but the proportion of HDL to LDL is also important. It helps to understand that HDLs clear cholesterol out of the body but LDLs deposit their share of the cholesterol on the walls of the cardiovascular system.

Research indicates that calories from fat should be limited to less than 30 percent of the daily caloric intake. Calories from saturated fats, such as those found in butter, cream, meat, fish, and poultry, should provide less than 10 percent of the daily fat intake.

With these facts in mind, Mrs. Cavaiani has provided recipes for familiar cakes and cookies without cholesterol and with reduced fat and sugar. It should be a welcome relief for those frustrated people who used to feel their households were turning into diet kitchens when dinnertime meant preparing two separate dinners, one for the dieter and one for the rest of the family.

Joseph T. Crockett, M.D., L.F.A.P.A.
San Diego, California

INTRODUCTION

As you use this book, you will notice that the title is *Cholesterol-free Cakes &*
Cookies, yet a few of the recipes have one or two milligrams of cholesterol
per serving. Since one or two milligrams of cholesterol is a very negligible
amount and the Food and Drug Administration has ruled that any food
that contains less than two milligrams of cholesterol and less than two
grams of saturated fat per serving may be considered cholesterol-free, I
have felt free to title the book "cholesterol-free."

I have lowered the amount of fat and sugar in the recipes. Most of the
recipes have had the fat and sugar cut by 50 percent, although this has not
been a hard-and-fast rule. However, the fat and sugar have been cut as
much as possible while still retaining the taste and texture of the original
cakes and cookies. These recipes are meant to add variety and appetite
appeal to your low-cholesterol diet without anyone else knowing that you
are using low-cholesterol recipes unless you tell them.

You probably bought or were given this book because you have been
following a low-cholesterol diet and are ready to try some good
cholesterol-free cakes and cookies to add variety to your diet. I'm sure you
know that following a low-cholesterol diet means substituting polyun-

saturated or monounsaturated vegetable fats for animal or saturated fats. This means you will need to use appropriate substitutes for the butter, lard, cream, eggs, whole milk, coconut, and chocolate chips in your cakes and cookies.

It is also important to reduce the total amount of fat and sugar in your diet. Research has shown that reducing the fat and sugar in your diet will help lower your total cholesterol, particularly the bad LDL (low-density lipoprotein) and triglycerides. The general rule is to keep fat to 30 percent of the total calories in your daily diet, with at least 20 percent from polyunsaturated or monounsaturated fats, and to cut down on sugar.

My major at Iowa State University was in experimental cookery, where we learned that fat and sugar can be cut in most recipes by 50 percent without ruining the final product. But this is not always true. Occasionally, you have to work with the recipe and prepare it several times to find out how much fat and sugar can be cut and still keep the taste and texture of the original cake or cookie. I have found that either margarine or vegetable oil will give good results, but if you want your cake or cookie to have a buttery taste, you'll need to add butter flavoring because you can't use butter in a low-cholesterol diet.

It is always important to read labels, but it is especially important to read them carefully when you are buying margarine. Ingredients are listed according to their percentage of the total product; that is, the ingredient with the largest percentage is listed first and the others are listed in order according to their percentages of the total product. There is always more of the first ingredient than there is the last. You should always look for margarine with vegetable oil as its first ingredient. Don't even consider buying margarine that lists beef fat or lard in the ingredient list.

The nutritive values of these recipes have been computed by the staff of the Fayette County, Iowa, Extension Service. Information used was based on a computer program developed by Dr. Elizabeth Shaffer, R.D., Iowa State University Extension Nutritionist. During the stage at which I was developing the recipes, and before the final computerization, I based my work on the information in the following publications:

U.S. Department of Agriculture. *Nutritive Value of American Foods in Common Units.* Agriculture Handbook No. 456. Washington, D.C.: Superintendent of Documents, U.S. Printing Office, 1975.

U.S. Department of Agriculture. *Nutritive Value of Foods.* Home and Garden Bulletin No. 72. Washington, D.C.: Superintendent of Documents, U.S. Printing Office, 1977.

U.S. Department of Agriculture. *Composition of Foods, Raw, Processed and Prepared.* Agriculture Handbook No. 8. Washington, D.C.: Superintendent of Documents, U.S. Printing Office, 1963 and all current revisions.

I hope you will use and enjoy these recipes and that they will help make your low-cholesterol diet more interesting. I'm sure your friends and family will never know you are serving them low-cholesterol foods unless you tell them, but you can feel proud that they are enjoying healthier desserts with you.

Mabel Cavaiani, R.D.
Wadena, Iowa

CAKES

CAKE
PREPARATION

THERE IS NO need to deprive yourself and your family of cake and cookies when you are restricted to a low-cholesterol diet. Many recipes can be easily adapted to your diet, allowing you to enjoy some delicious treats even after the fat and sugar content in the original recipe has been cut in half.

Our family doctor told my husband to follow a low-cholesterol diet. At that time there were very few low-cholesterol recipes available, so we followed a pretty restricted diet. After a few months I realized I could adapt many of our favorite recipes so we could have them again. At first we didn't worry about the fat and sugar content. We were just happy to bring his cholesterol count down to normal. When we realized that controlling the amount of sugar and fat in the diet was also important, I started adapting my recipes all over again. I'm happy to say that most of them were easy to do and I ended up with some recipes that I think are really good. I hope you will enjoy them also and use them to make your own low-cholesterol diet more interesting.

Adapting recipes is simply a matter of substituting low-cholesterol foods for high-cholesterol foods. You can use dry buttermilk and vegetable oil instead of sour cream, margarine in place of butter, and egg whites or liquid egg substitute instead of whole eggs.

Regular sour cream is generally 33 percent butterfat and 67 percent buttermilk. To adapt 1 cup sour cream to a cholesterol-free diet, I would use 1/3 cup oil and 2/3 cup sour milk or buttermilk. However, to adapt it to a reduced-fat diet, I would cut the fat to 2 or 3 tablespoons instead of ¹/₃ cup oil and keep the amount of sour milk or buttermilk at ²/₃ cup. It is important to use the sour milk or buttermilk because most recipes that use sour cream use baking soda for leavening, and baking soda needs the sour milk or buttermilk to react properly.

Chocolate contains cocoa butter, which is high in cholesterol. Dry cocoa doesn't contain cocoa butter, so it can be used as a substitute for chocolate. Three tablespoons dry cocoa and 1 tablespoon fat will substitute for a 1-ounce square of chocolate. If I can, I just use the cocoa and eliminate the fat.

Liquid egg substitute is wonderful and can be used instead of whole eggs in most recipes. Liquid egg substitute can't be used in many European-style cakes in which the eggs are beaten for a long time, but it is very good for most cakes, giving the same flavor and results as whole eggs. Of course there are some recipes such as angel food cake in which we have always used egg whites.

You will note that I have measured the egg whites and liquid egg substitute in most of these recipes because doing that is the most accurate way to bake. For other cooking purposes, two large egg whites equal ¹/₄ cup egg whites. I buy the large or extra-large eggs because I'd rather use those than have to crack so many small eggs for my egg whites.

I nearly always use instant nonfat dry milk for fresh skim milk and dry buttermilk for fresh low-fat buttermilk. I like the fact that instant nonfat dry milk is virtually cholesterol-free and dry buttermilk has very little cholesterol. (Whole skim milk is *almost* cholesterol-free.) I also like the fact that dry milks are less expensive, keep for a long time, and are easy to use. I do not reconstitute these dried milk products when I bake. I just stir the powder in with the flour and add the equivalent amount of water to the liquid. As you begin baking these recipes, you will note that the proportion of liquid to dry milk is not always constant. I did that for specific reasons: If I wanted a cake with fewer calories, I cut the amount of milk. If I wanted a milkier taste, I added more milk. When you are adapting your own recipes, you can begin by following the proportions for preparing liquid milk on the package. Instant nonfat dry milk can be kept at room temperature, but dry buttermilk should be refrigerated after the container is opened.

The fat in cake and cookie recipes is important for flavor and tenderness. Margarine can be substituted for butter on a one-to-one basis. When you buy margarine, be careful to purchase only margarine that lists vegetable oil as the first ingredient. Also, margarine should be refrigerated when it isn't being used. I find that soft margarine is good for table use but not all that good for baking, so I always use stick margarine for baking. I always substitute margarine for butter, lard, or shortening if it is going to be creamed and vegetable oil if the fat is going to be melted before it is used. I use vegetable oil whenever possible in these recipes. Some recipes, though, use margarine because margarine gives the cake a better texture.

All-purpose flour is used instead of cake flour in most of these recipes because it gives a firmer texture, more like a European cake, which I prefer. I stir together flour and other dry ingredients instead of sifting them because stirring is much easier and gives the results of blending and aerating the mixture.

Of course, there are certain basic rules you must follow when preparing any cakes:

1. Follow directions carefully. It is a good idea to read the recipe and assemble the equipment and ingredients before you start working. It can be a disaster if you start preparing a recipe and discover you don't have the right ingredients or equipment halfway through the recipe. It is also important to follow the mixing directions and baking time and temperature exactly.

2. Always use standard measuring cups and spoons and the baking pans indicated in the recipe. Batter will overflow if the pan is too small and it will bake into a thin, hard cake if the pan is too large. I use metal cake pans for all my baking. If you use glass pans, reduce the heat listed in the recipe by 25 degrees. The use of non-stick pans will simplify your baking. It is much easier to remove a coffee cake, or any kind of a cake, from a non-stick pan that has been sprayed with cooking spray or

greased with margarine than it is from a pan without a non-stick surface. If you are cutting a cake in a non-stick pan, you need to use a plastic knife.

3. Always use good-quality, fresh ingredients and never make substitutions without knowing the exact substitution rate. All ingredients should be at room temperature unless the directions indicate otherwise. Eggs, liquid egg substitute, and margarine should be refrigerated. Then they should be allowed to come to room temperature just before they are used. Flour should be refrigerated if it isn't going to be used regularly; it, too, should be allowed to come to room temperature before it is used. Instant nonfat dry milk can be kept at room temperature if it is used frequently. If it is used only occasionally it should be stored in the refrigerator or freezer. Dry buttermilk should be refrigerated after the package is opened, but unopened packages may be stored at room temperature. Dry milks should be refrigerated once they are mixed with water.

4. Always preheat the oven to the temperature indicated in the recipe before baking.

5. When baking a single cake, put it in the center of the rack in the center of the oven. When baking cake layers, put them on the same rack, if possible, being careful to leave room around them to allow the hot air to circulate.

6. Don't open the oven door while the cake is baking unless it is absolutely necessary. Most cakes can be tested by inserting a cake tester or a toothpick in the center. The tester will come out clean when the cake is baked. Cakes generally pull away from the sides of the pan when they are baked and spring back when touched lightly in the center. If the cake isn't done in the specified time, return it to the oven for another 5 minutes before testing it again. When the cakes are done, cool them on wire racks away from drafts for best results.

7. Most cakes freeze well. I put them, uncovered, on a plate in the freezer for about an hour and then wrap them in freezer paper, freezer-safe plastic, or aluminum foil and return to the freezer. When I defrost them, I remove the protective covering, put them on a plate again, and set

them in the refrigerator overnight. You can also put cakes in a cake saver to defrost at room temperature, but you want to be sure that they can't pick up moisture from the air in the room while they are defrosting. Sometimes I cut a cake before it is frozen and then remove the cake a couple of pieces at a time.

CHOCOLATE

CAKES

CHOCOLATE APPLESAUCE CAKE

CHERRY CHOCOLATE CAKE

COCOMINT CAKE

DANISH DEVIL'S FOOD CAKE

FUDGE CAKE

IOWA SMOOTH-AS-SILK CAKE

CHOCOLATE KRAUT CAKE

MARASCHINO CHERRY CAKE

DEEP DARK CHOCOLATE CAKE

LOW-SUGAR CHOCOLATE CAKE

MOCHA NUT CAKE

CHOCOLATE NUT CAKE

CHOCOLATE RAISIN CAKE

CHOCOLATE DATE CAKE

CHOCOLATE POTATO LOAF

LET'S FACE IT. There are millions of chocoholics in this country, and I'm one of them. Most other cakes and cookies seem pale and uninteresting to us when compared to a rich chocolate cake or cookie.

Of course, we cannot use pure chocolate on a low-cholesterol diet because it contains cocoa butter, which is high in saturated fat. But a cake or cookie made with cocoa can be just as luscious and appealing as anything made with pure chocolate. As noted in Cake Preparation (page 4), 3 tablespoons of cocoa and 1 tablespoon of margarine or oil is equal to 1 ounce of chocolate, and few people can tell the difference.

When cocoa is substituted for chocolate, the cocoa is generally mixed in with the flour and the fat is added to the fat in the recipe. You can omit that added fat if you wish, but you will get a richer product if you keep it. Sometimes you can use a little hot water mixed in with the cocoa to give you a mixture more closely resembling chocolate; for these recipes, however, it isn't generally necessary.

Some people say that the caffeine in chocolate and cocoa is why it is so popular, but I think it is the aroma and flavor that make so many people love it.

More people are now using chocolate cakes for their weddings or cakes with a chocolate layer and a white layer. Caterers tell me no one is surprised when the wedding cake is chocolate.

If you have a white or yellow cake that you really like but wish were chocolate, you can try substituting $1/3$ cup of cocoa for $1/3$ cup of flour for a 9 by 13-inch cake or two 9-inch layers. If that isn't enough chocolate for you, increase the cocoa to $1/2$ cup.

Vanilla has been the favorite flavor with chocolate since chocolate was first discovered in Central America, but other flavors such as cherry or rum also accent chocolate. You can soak the layers of a chocolate cake with a little liqueur, but keep it to a minimum. Too much liqueur will ruin the taste and texture of the cake.

Nutritive values for the cakes are for the cakes alone, unless the ingredients for the frosting or the exact amount of frosting is included in the list of ingredients. When the frosting is not listed in the ingredients, the nutritive values for the frosting should be added to the nutritive values for the cake. There are several recipes in Frostings and Sauces that go well with chocolate cakes. I like Chocolate Fudge Frosting (page 182), but others may prefer Vanilla Buttercream Frosting (page 190) or Vanilla Powdered Sugar Frosting (page 192). Whether you eat your chocolate cake plain or with frosting or a topping, enjoy it with a clear conscience, knowing that all of the recipes in this book are cholesterol-free and contain less sugar and fat than most chocolate cakes.

If you are new to baking, please read the seven basic rules for cake baking in Cake Preparation (page 5) before making any of the cakes in this chapter.

CHOCOLATE APPLESAUCE CAKE

This cake is much lighter than the traditional applesauce cake. It may be baked in a single square pan or used for a layer cake.

YIELD: ONE 9-INCH SQUARE CAKE OR TWO 8-INCH ROUND LAYERS

½ cup (1 stick) margarine

¾ cup sugar

½ cup egg whites or liquid egg substitute, at room temperature

1 teaspoon vanilla extract

2 cups all-purpose flour

¼ cup cocoa

1 teaspoon baking soda

½ teaspoon salt

1 teaspoon cinnamon

1 cup unsweetened applesauce, at room temperature

Preheat oven to 350°F. Grease a 9-inch square cake pan with margarine or cooking spray and set aside.

Using an electric mixer at medium speed, cream margarine and sugar together until light and fluffy. Add egg whites or liquid egg substitute and vanilla and mix at medium speed until smooth and creamy, scraping down the bowl before and after the addition.

Stir flour, cocoa, baking soda, salt, and cinnamon together to blend and then add, along with the applesauce, to the creamy mixture. Mix at medium speed until creamy.

Spread the batter evenly in the prepared pan. Bake for 30 to 35 minutes or until the cake pulls away from the sides of the pan and a cake tester inserted in the center comes out clean.

For a layer cake, spread half of the batter in each of two greased, waxed paper–lined 8-inch layer cake pans and bake for 20 to 25 minutes.

Cool on a wire rack. Frost if desired.

NUTRITIVE VALUES PER SERVING

Number of servings 16

calories 157 • carbohydrate 24 grams • protein 3 grams • fat 6 grams
sodium 197 milligrams • cholesterol 0 milligrams

Low-sodium diets: Omit salt
and use salt-free margarine.

CHERRY CHOCOLATE CAKE

Many people prepare this with cake mix but I like it better made from scratch.

YIELD: ONE 9 BY 13-INCH CAKE

3 cups (⅓ pound) miniature marshmallows

½ cup (1 stick) margarine

¾ cup sugar

1 large egg white or 2 tablespoons liquid egg substitute

1 teaspoon vanilla extract

1½ cups all-purpose flour

⅓ cup cocoa

1 teaspoon baking powder

½ teaspoon baking soda

¼ teaspoon salt

¾ cup water, at room temperature

1 21-ounce can cherry pie filling

Preheat oven to 350°F. Grease a 9 by 13-inch cake pan with margarine. Then sprinkle the marshmallows evenly over the bottom of the pan and set aside.

Using an electric mixer at medium speed, cream margarine and sugar together until light and fluffy. Add egg white or liquid egg substitute and vanilla and mix at medium speed until creamy, scraping down the bowl before and after the addition.

Stir flour, cocoa, baking powder, baking soda, and salt together to blend well and add, along with the water, to the creamy mixture. Mix at medium speed until smooth.

Spread the batter evenly over the marshmallows. Dot with the cherry pie filling. Bake for 35 to 40 minutes or until the cake pulls away from the sides of the pan and the cake portion springs back when touched. Cool on a wire rack.

NUTRITIVE VALUES PER SERVING

Number of servings 16

calories 200 • carbohydrate 35 grams • protein 3 grams • fat 6 grams
sodium 127 milligrams • cholesterol 0 milligrams

Low-sodium diets: Omit salt.
Use salt-free margarine and low-sodium baking powder.

COCOMINT CAKE

For this recipe it is important to use hard sugar peppermints with red stripes on them and to crush them until they are as fine as sugar. I use my food processor to crush them because it is quicker and easier than doing it by hand.

*YIELD: ONE 9 BY 13-INCH CAKE OR TWO
9-INCH ROUND LAYERS*

1/3 cup hard striped peppermints

1 cup sugar

2/3 cup (1 1/3 sticks) margarine

1/2 cup egg whites or liquid egg substitute

2 1/4 cups all-purpose flour

2/3 cup cocoa

1 teaspoon baking powder

1 teaspoon baking soda

1/2 teaspoon salt

1/4 cup instant nonfat dry milk

1 1/3 cups water, at room temperature

Preheat oven to 350°F. Grease a 9 by 13-inch cake pan with margarine or cooking spray and set aside.

Crush peppermints to a fine powder and place in the bowl of an electric mixer, along with the sugar and margarine. Cream at medium speed until light and fluffy. Add egg whites or liquid egg substitute and mix at medium speed until creamy, scraping down the bowl before and after the addition.

Stir flour, cocoa, baking powder, baking soda, salt, and dry milk together to blend well. Add to the creamed mixture, along with the water, and beat at medium speed until smooth.

Pour the batter into the prepared pan. Bake for 40 minutes or until the cake pulls away from the sides of the pan and a cake tester inserted in the center comes out clean.

For a layer cake, pour half of the batter into each of two greased 9-inch round cake pans and bake for 25 to 30 minutes.

Cool cakes on a wire rack. Frost if desired.

NUTRITIVE VALUES PER SERVING

Number of servings 20

---

calories 168 • carbohydrate 26 grams • protein 3 grams • fat 6 grams
sodium 194 milligrams • cholesterol 0 milligrams

Low-sodium diets: Omit salt.
Use salt-free margarine and low-sodium baking powder.

DANISH DEVIL'S FOOD CAKE

This is a leaner version of a wonderful Danish cake. To give it a special touch I sometimes soak it with three or four tablespoons of chocolate liqueur before frosting it.

YIELD: ONE 9-INCH SQUARE CAKE

²/₃ cup cocoa

2 cups all-purpose flour

1¼ cups sugar

¼ cup dry buttermilk

1 teaspoon baking soda

½ teaspoon salt

1²/₃ cups water, at room temperature

½ cup egg whites

¹/₃ cup vegetable oil

1 teaspoon vanilla extract

Preheat oven to 350°F. Grease a 9-inch square cake pan with margarine or cooking spray and set aside.

Place cocoa, flour, sugar, dry buttermilk, baking soda, and salt in the bowl of an electric mixer and mix at low speed to blend well.

Stir water, egg whites, oil, and vanilla together with a fork to blend and then add to the dry mixture. Beat at medium speed for 1½ minutes. Pour the batter into the prepared pan. Bake for 40 to 45 minutes or until the cake pulls away from the sides of the pan and a cake tester inserted in the center comes out clean. Cool on a wire rack. Frost if desired.

NUTRITIVE VALUES PER SERVING

Number of servings 16

---

calories 177 • carbohydrate 30 grams • protein 4 grams • fat 5 grams
sodium 141 milligrams • cholesterol 1 milligram

Low-sodium diets: Omit salt.

FUDGE CAKE

This is the cake young ladies served their best beaux and older women served their club ladies in the early 1900s. It is a fine-textured, moist cake, which can be baked in a flat pan or made into layers and served with a fluffy frosting.

YIELD: ONE 9 BY 13-INCH CAKE OR TWO 9-INCH LAYERS

³/₄ cup (1¹/₂ sticks) margarine

1 cup brown sugar

¹/₃ cup cocoa

¹/₄ cup hot water

¹/₂ cup egg whites or liquid egg substitute

2 cups all-purpose flour

1 teaspoon baking soda

1 tablespoon vinegar

1 teaspoon vanilla extract

Water as needed, at room temperature

Preheat oven to 350°F. Grease a 9 by 13-inch cake pan with margarine or cooking spray and set aside.

Using an electric mixer at medium speed, cream margarine and brown sugar together until light and fluffy.

Combine cocoa and hot water and stir until smooth. Add to creamed mixture, along with egg whites or liquid egg substitute. Mix until creamy, scraping down the bowl before and after the addition.

Stir flour and baking soda together and set aside. Pour vinegar and vanilla into a 1-cup measure and fill with water.

Add the flour mixture, then the water mixture, to the creamed mixture and mix at medium speed for 30 seconds or until smooth and well blended.

Pour the batter into the prepared pan. Bake for 35 to 40 minutes or until the cake is firm in the center and pulls away from the sides of the pan.

For a layer cake, pour half of the batter into each of two greased 9-inch cake pans and bake for about 30 minutes. Frost if desired.

NUTRITIVE VALUES PER SERVING

Number of servings 20

---

calories 153 • carbohydrate 21 grams • protein 2 grams • fat 7 grams
sodium 135 milligrams • cholesterol 0 milligrams

Low-sodium diets: Use salt-free margarine.

IOWA SMOOTH-AS-SILK CAKE

My friend Mildred "Cracker" Holton from Clearwater, Florida, brought this recipe to me when she came up for a visit last summer. Her recipe was called "Texas Cake," but when I got through changing it to fit a low-cholesterol diet, she suggested I change the name as well, to recognize the state where we worked on it. She says it tastes like her cake but now she can eat it with a clear conscience.

YIELD: ONE 11 BY 15-INCH CAKE

CAKE

¼ cup (½ stick) margarine

⅓ cup cocoa

1 cup water

¼ cup vegetable oil

1 teaspoon vanilla extract

1 tablespoon white vinegar

2 cups all-purpose flour

1½ cups sugar

2 tablespoons instant nonfat dry milk

1 teaspoon baking soda

½ teaspoon salt

1 teaspoon cinnamon

½ cup liquid egg substitute

FROSTING

¼ cup water

¼ cup cocoa

2 tablespoons (¼ stick) margarine

2 cups powdered or confectioners' sugar

1 teaspoon vanilla extract

¼ cup chopped English walnuts

Preheat oven to 350°F. Grease an 11 by 15-inch jelly roll pan with margarine or cooking spray and set aside.

Combine margarine, cocoa, and water in a saucepan or microwave-safe bowl. Cook over low heat or in a microwave until the margarine is melted. Remove from the heat and stir in oil, vanilla, and vinegar. Set aside.

While the mixture is heating, place the flour, sugar, dry milk, baking soda, salt, and cinnamon in the bowl of an electric mixer and mix at low speed to blend well. Add the liquid egg substitute and the warm cocoa mixture and mix at medium speed for 1 minute.

Pour the batter into the prepared pan. Bake for 20 minutes or until the cake pulls away from the sides of the pan and the center springs back when touched. Cool on a wire rack.

As soon as the cake is removed from the oven, prepare the frosting: Combine the water, cocoa, and margarine in a saucepan or microwave-safe bowl. Heat on the stovetop or in the microwave oven until the margarine is melted. Remove from the heat and add the powdered sugar, vanilla, and nuts. Beat until glossy. Then pour the frosting evenly over the warm cake. Cool to room temperature before cutting.

NUTRITIVE VALUES PER SERVING

Number of servings 24

---

calories 181 • carbohydrate 32 grams • protein 2 grams • fat 6 grams
sodium 113 milligrams • cholesterol 0 milligrams

Low-sodium diets: Omit salt
and use salt-free margarine.

CHOCOLATE KRAUT CAKE

This tastes so much like coconut cake that no one will guess those shreds are sauerkraut and not coconut.

YIELD: ONE 9 BY 13-INCH CAKE

²/₃ cup (1¹/₃ sticks) margarine

1 cup sugar

¹/₂ cup egg whites or liquid egg substitute

1 teaspoon coconut flavoring

2 cups all-purpose flour

¹/₂ cup cocoa

1 teaspoon baking powder

1 teaspoon baking soda

¹/₂ teaspoon salt

1 cup water, at room temperature

¹/₂ cup well-drained, chopped sauerkraut

Preheat oven to 375°F. Grease a 9 by 13-inch cake pan with margarine or cooking spray and set aside.

Using an electric mixer at medium speed, cream margarine and sugar together until light and fluffy. Add egg whites or liquid egg substitute and coconut flavoring and mix at medium speed until light and creamy, scraping down the bowl before and after the addition.

Stir flour, cocoa, baking powder, baking soda, and salt together to blend well. Add to the creamy mixture, along with the water, and beat at medium speed until smooth. Stir in the sauerkraut.

Spread the batter evenly in the prepared pan. Bake for 35 minutes or until the cake pulls away from the sides of the pan and a cake tester inserted in the center comes out clean. Cool on a wire rack. Frost if desired.

NUTRITIVE VALUES PER SERVING

Number of servings 20

---

calories 144 • carbohydrate 20 grams • protein 2 grams • fat 6 grams
sodium 230 milligrams • cholesterol 0 milligrams

Low-sodium diets: Omit salt.
Use salt-free margarine and low-sodium baking powder.

MARASCHINO CHERRY CAKE

YIELD: ONE 9-INCH SQUARE CAKE

1 cup water

1/3 cup maraschino cherry juice

1 teaspoon cherry flavoring

1/2 cup (1 stick) margarine

1/2 cup sugar

Dry sugar substitute equal to
    1/4 cup sugar (optional)

1/4 cup egg whites or liquid egg
    substitute

2 cups all-purpose flour

1/4 cup cocoa

2 tablespoons instant nonfat
    dry milk

1 teaspoon baking powder

1 teaspoon baking soda

1/2 teaspoon salt

1/2 cup well-drained, chopped
    maraschino cherries

Preheat oven to 350°F. Grease a 9-inch square cake pan with margarine
or cooking spray and set aside.

Combine water, cherry juice, and flavoring and set aside.

Using an electric mixer at medium speed, cream margarine, sugar, and sugar substitute together until light and fluffy. Add egg whites or liquid egg substitute and mix at medium speed until creamy, scraping down the bowl before and after the addition.

Stir flour, cocoa, dry milk, baking powder, baking soda, and salt together to blend. Then add, along with the liquid mixture, to the creamy mixture. Mix at medium speed until creamy. Stir in the cherries.

Spread the batter evenly in the prepared pan. Bake 45 minutes or until the cake pulls away from the sides of the pan and a cake tester inserted in the center comes out clean. Frost if desired.

NUTRITIVE VALUES PER SERVING

Number of servings 16

---

calories 154 • carbohydrate 23 grams • protein 2 grams • fat 6 grams
sodium 214 milligrams • cholesterol 0 milligrams

Low-sodium diets: Omit salt.
Use salt-free margarine and low-sodium baking powder.

DEEP DARK CHOCOLATE CAKE

This recipe is based on one that appeared in an advertisement for Hershey's cocoa many years ago. It is the darkest, richest cocoa cake I've ever seen. It tastes like it is loaded with chocolate, but we know it is made with cocoa.

*YIELD: ONE 9 BY 13-INCH CAKE OR TWO
9-INCH LAYERS*

1³/₄ cups all-purpose flour

1 cup sugar

³/₄ cup cocoa

²/₃ cup instant nonfat dry milk

1¹/₂ teaspoons baking powder

1¹/₂ teaspoons baking soda

¹/₂ teaspoon salt

1 cup water, at room temperature

¹/₂ cup egg whites or liquid egg substitute

¹/₂ cup vegetable oil

2 teaspoons vanilla extract

³/₄ cup boiling water

Preheat oven to 350°F. Grease a 9 by 13-inch cake pan with margarine or cooking spray and set aside.

Place flour, sugar, cocoa, dry milk, baking powder, baking soda, and salt in the bowl of an electric mixer and mix at low speed for 30 seconds or until well blended. Beat 1 cup water, egg whites or liquid egg substitute, oil, and vanilla together and add to the flour mixture. Mix at medium speed for 2 minutes. Add boiling water and mix to blend.

Pour the batter into the prepared pan. Bake for 30 minutes or until the cake starts to pull away from the sides of the pan and a cake tester inserted in the center comes out clean.

For a layer cake, pour the batter into two greased 9-inch layer cake pans. Bake 20 to 25 minutes.

Cool in the pan for 10 minutes. Then turn out onto a wire rack to cool to room temperature. Frost with White Mountain Frosting (page 188) if desired, although the nutritive values are for the serving of cake alone.

NUTRITIVE VALUES PER SERVING

Number of servings 16

---

calories 174 • carbohydrate 26 grams • protein 3 grams • fat 7 grams
sodium 196 milligrams • cholesterol 1 milligram

Low-sodium diets: Omit salt
and use low-sodium baking powder.

LOW-SUGAR CHOCOLATE CAKE

This delicious cake is not only low in sugar, it is also high in fiber. To give the cake a light texture, it is important to soak the bran with the other ingredients as directed so that the cereal will dissolve in the batter.

YIELD: ONE 9-INCH SQUARE CAKE OR 12 CUPCAKES

1 cup 100% Bran, Bran Buds, All Bran, or Fiber One cereal

1 cup water

Dry sugar substitute equal to $^1/_3$ cup sugar

$^1/_4$ cup egg whites or liquid egg substitute

$^1/_4$ cup vegetable oil

1 teaspoon vanilla extract

1 teaspoon chocolate flavoring (optional)

1 tablespoon lemon juice

1 cup all-purpose flour

$^1/_4$ cup cocoa

$^1/_4$ cup sugar

2 tablespoons instant nonfat dry milk

1 teaspoon baking soda

$^1/_2$ teaspoon salt

$^1/_2$ teaspoon cinnamon

Preheat oven to 350°F. Grease a 9-inch square cake pan with margarine or cooking spray and set aside.

Place bran cereal, water, sugar substitute, egg whites or liquid egg substitute, oil, flavorings, and lemon juice in the bowl of an electric mixer. Mix lightly and let stand at room temperature for 45 minutes.

Combine flour, cocoa, sugar, dry milk, baking soda, salt, and cinnamon and stir to blend. Add to the bran mixture and mix at medium speed for 30 seconds or until well blended.

Pour the batter into the prepared pan. Bake for 20 to 25 minutes or until the cake pulls away from the sides of the pan and a cake tester inserted in the center comes out clean. Cool before serving.

NOTE: This batter also makes excellent cupcakes. Grease a 12-cup muffin tin with margarine or cooking spray, or line with paper liners. Fill cups with batter about halfway (or use a level No. 20 dipper) and bake for 15 to 20 minutes.

NUTRITIVE VALUES PER SERVING

Number of servings 12

---

calories 111 • carbohydrate 15 grams • protein 2 grams • fat 5 grams
sodium 197 milligrams • cholesterol 0 milligrams

Low-sodium diets: Omit salt.

MOCHA NUT CAKE

YIELD: ONE 9-INCH SQUARE CAKE

¾ cup very hot water

1 tablespoon instant coffee

¾ cup chopped Brazil nuts

2 tablespoons sugar

½ cup (1 stick) margarine

¾ cup brown sugar

1 egg white or 2 tablespoons
liquid egg substitute

1 teaspoon vanilla extract

1½ cups all-purpose flour

⅓ cup cocoa

¼ cup instant nonfat dry milk

2 teaspoons baking powder

¼ teaspoon salt

Preheat oven to 350°F. Grease a 9-inch square cake pan with margarine or cooking spray and set aside.

Combine hot water and instant coffee and stir to dissolve coffee. Set aside. Combine ¼ cup nuts and sugar and set aside.

Using an electric mixer at medium speed, cream margarine and brown sugar together until light and fluffy. Add egg white or liquid egg substitute and vanilla and mix at medium speed until smooth, scraping down the bowl before and after the addition.

Stir flour, cocoa, dry milk, baking powder, salt, and remaining ½ cup nuts together to blend. Add, along with the reserved coffee mixture, to the creamed mixture. Mix at medium speed until smooth.

Spread the batter evenly in the prepared pan. Sprinkle the reserved nut and sugar mixture evenly over the top of the cake batter, pressing it down lightly with the back of a large tablespoon. Bake for 30 minutes or until the cake pulls away from the sides of the pan and a cake tester inserted in the center comes out clean. Cool on a wire rack. Frost if desired.

NUTRITIVE VALUES PER SERVING

Number of servings 16

---

calories 182 • carbohydrate 23 grams • protein 3 grams • fat 9 grams
sodium 154 milligrams • cholesterol 0 milligrams

Low-sodium diets: Omit salt.
Use salt-free margarine and low-sodium baking powder.

CHOCOLATE NUT CAKE

This simple, delicious cake proves that it is possible to make good desserts without eggs.

YIELD: ONE 9-INCH SQUARE CAKE

1½ cups all-purpose flour

½ cup sugar

¼ cup cocoa

1 teaspoon baking soda

¼ teaspoon salt

1 cup water, at room temperature

⅓ cup vegetable oil

1 teaspoon vanilla extract

1 tablespoon lemon juice

¼ cup chopped English walnuts

Preheat oven to 350°F. Grease a 9-inch square cake pan with margarine or cooking spray and set aside.

Place flour, sugar, cocoa, baking soda, and salt in the bowl of an electric mixer and mix at low speed to blend well.

Combine water, oil, vanilla, and lemon juice and mix well with a fork. Add to the flour mixture and mix at medium speed to blend well. Stir in the nuts. Pour the batter into the prepared pan. Bake for 30 to 35 minutes or until the cake pulls away from the sides of the pan and a cake tester inserted in the center comes out clean. Cool, then frost if desired.

VARIATIONS

1. CHOCOLATE RAISIN CAKE: Omit the nuts and add ½ cup raisins to the flour mixture.

2. CHOCOLATE DATE CAKE: Omit the nuts and add ½ cup chopped dates to the flour mixture.

NUTRITIVE VALUES PER SERVING

Number of servings 12

---

calories 166 • carbohydrate 22 grams • protein 3 grams • fat 8 grams
sodium 118 milligrams • cholesterol 0 milligrams

Low-sodium diets: Omit salt.

CHOCOLATE POTATO LOAF

This recipe was made originally with mashed potatoes, but this method is much simpler and the texture is better.

YIELD: ONE 9 BY 5 BY 3-INCH LOAF CAKE

½ cup (1 stick) margarine

1 cup sugar

½ cup egg whites or liquid egg substitute, at room temperature

2 teaspoons vanilla extract

2 cups all-purpose flour

½ cup instant potato flakes or buds

½ cup cocoa

2 tablespoons instant nonfat dry milk

1 tablespoon baking powder

½ teaspoon salt

1 teaspoon cinnamon

1¼ cups water, at room temperature

Preheat oven to 350°F. Grease a 9 by 5 by 3-inch loaf pan with margarine or cooking spray and set aside.

Using an electric mixer at medium speed, cream margarine and sugar together until light and fluffy. Add egg whites or liquid egg substitute and vanilla and mix at medium speed for 30 seconds, scraping down the bowl before and after the addition.

Stir flour, potato flakes or buds, cocoa, dry milk, baking powder, salt, and cinnamon together and add to the egg mixture, along with the water. Mix at medium speed until creamy. Let the batter rest for 2 minutes in the bowl. Then mix again briefly.

Spread the batter evenly in the prepared pan. Bake for 50 to 60 minutes or until a cake tester inserted in the center comes out clean. Cool in the pan for 10 minutes. Then turn out onto a wire rack to cool to room temperature.

NUTRITIVE VALUES PER SERVING

Number of servings 16

calories 176 • carbohydrate 27 grams • protein 3 grams • fat 7 grams
sodium 232 milligrams • cholesterol 0 milligrams

Low-sodium diets: Omit salt.
Use salt-free margarine and low-sodium baking powder.
Substitute ³/₄ cup salt-free mashed potatoes
for the instant potatoes and ¹/₄ cup of the water.

CAKES WITH
FRUIT

APPLE OAT BRAN CAKE

DARK APPLESAUCE RAISIN CAKE

LIGHT APPLESAUCE CAKE

APPLESAUCE WALNUT RAISIN CAKE

APPLESAUCE GRAHAM CAKE

BANANA DATE CAKE

DATE NUT CAKE

APRICOT ALMOND CAKE

THE FIRST SPRING CAKE

FRUIT COCKTAIL CAKE

JAM CAKE

JAM NUT CAKE

RAISIN JAM CAKE

PINEAPPLE CARROT CAKE

PRUNE CAKE

STRAWBERRY PECAN CAKE

IN THE DEAD of winter cakes made with fruit seem to bring back a breath of summer or fall. Fruit adds color, texture, and flavor to cakes. It is fat- and cholesterol-free (except for coconut), high in fiber, and low in calories — truly a paragon among foods.

I've used fresh, canned, or frozen fruit in these recipes and have tried to use sugar-free or low-sugar fruits whenever possible to help reduce the sugar content of the recipes. Jam is used in the jam cake, but even that cake has only a moderate amount of sugar in it.

Fruit has a high moisture content, so you need to remember that you are adding almost the same amount of liquid as fruit. You have probably noticed that very little liquid is added to an applesauce cake because applesauce has such a high moisture content. This is true of most fruits, with the exception of dried or candied fruits, such as dates, raisins, or candied cherries. They have a lower moisture content and are added to the batter, not part of the batter.

Cakes with a high percentage of fruit, such as The First Spring Cake (page 45), do not keep well because of their high moisture content. They are luscious the first day but soggy the next. If I don't serve all of the cake the first day, I freeze it immediately in a plastic freezer bag or in aluminum foil and defrost it in my microwave oven or overnight in the refrigerator when I want to serve it again.

Most fruit cakes don't need to be frosted, but occasionally it is nice to serve them with Custard Sauce (page 200) or Lemon or Orange Sauce (page 201). They go with most menus and add a nice touch to a low-fat, low-sugar, low-cholesterol diet.

Please review the seven basic rules for cake baking in Cake Preparation (page 5) before making any of the cakes in this chapter.

APPLE OAT BRAN CAKE

This combination of two high-fiber foods makes a delicious, nutritious cake.

YIELD: ONE 9 BY 13-INCH CAKE

2 cups coarsely grated apples (3 medium)

1 tablespoon lemon juice

2½ cups all-purpose flour

1 cup oat bran cereal

1¼ cups brown sugar

¼ cup instant nonfat dry milk

2 teaspoons cinnamon

1 teaspoon baking powder

1 teaspoon baking soda

½ teaspoon salt

½ cup raisins

1 cup water, at room temperature

½ cup vegetable oil

2 large egg whites or ¼ cup liquid egg substitute

Preheat oven to 375°F. Grease a 9 by 13-inch cake pan with margarine or cooking spray and set aside.

Sprinkle the coarsely grated apples with lemon juice and set aside.

Place flour, cereal, brown sugar, dry milk, cinnamon, baking powder, baking soda, salt, and raisins in the bowl of an electric mixer and mix at low speed to blend. Stir water, oil, and egg whites or liquid egg substitute together to blend and add, along with the apples, to the flour mixture. Mix at medium speed until creamy.

Spread the batter in the prepared pan. Bake for 35 to 40 minutes or until the cake pulls away from the sides of the pan and a cake tester inserted in the center comes out clean. Cool on a wire rack. Frost if desired.

NUTRITIVE VALUES PER SERVING

Number of servings 20

---

calories 200 • carbohydrate 34 grams • protein 3 grams • fat 6 grams
sodium 128 milligrams • cholesterol 0 milligrams

Low-sodium diets: Omit salt
and use low-sodium baking powder.

DARK APPLESAUCE RAISIN CAKE

This recipe is from my friend Beverly Wolfrum of Aurora, Colorado. She told me she started making it for special occasions when her husband, retired Episcopalian Bishop "Dub" Wolfrum, was in the seminary. Note that the baking soda is added to the applesauce, as our grandmothers used to do, not to the flour mixture, as most cookbooks today recommend. Trust me, this old-fashioned way works best with this cake.

YIELD: ONE 9 BY 5 BY 3-INCH LOAF CAKE

2 cups all-purpose flour

1 cup sugar

1 teaspoon cinnamon

1/2 teaspoon nutmeg

1/4 teaspoon ground cloves

1 1/2 cups hot, unsweetened
   applesauce

2 teaspoons baking soda

1/2 cup vegetable oil

1/2 cup chopped English walnuts

1/2 cup golden raisins

Preheat oven to 350°F. Grease a 9 by 5 by 3-inch, non-stick loaf pan with margarine or cooking spray. (If the loaf pan doesn't have a non-stick surface, grease it well, line with waxed paper, and grease again.) Set aside.

Place flour, sugar, cinnamon, nutmeg, and cloves in the bowl of an electric mixer and mix at low speed to blend well. Combine the applesauce and baking soda, mix lightly, and add to the flour mixture, along with the oil, nuts, and raisins. Mix at medium speed until the flour is moistened and the batter is creamy.

Spread the batter evenly in the prepared pan. Bake for 50 to 60 minutes or until a cake tester inserted in the center comes out clean. If the cake starts to brown too quickly, cover it loosely with aluminum foil. Cool in the pan on a wire rack for 10 to 15 minutes. Then turn out onto the rack, remove the waxed paper, and cool to room temperature.

NUTRITIVE VALUES PER SERVING

Number of servings 16

---

calories 213 • carbohydrate 31 grams • protein 2 grams • fat 9 grams
sodium 105 milligrams • cholesterol 0 milligrams

Low-sodium diets: Recipe may be used as written.

LIGHT APPLESAUCE CAKE

I took my mother to visit her cousin several years ago, and while they were talking I amused myself by going through her cousin's collection of old cookbooks. This recipe appeared in one of those books, which was written at the turn of the century as a promotional piece for a flour company. I tried the recipe and we all enjoyed it so much I added it to my own recipe file.

YIELD: ONE 9-INCH SQUARE CAKE

1 cup sugar

½ cup (1 stick) margarine

¼ cup egg whites or liquid egg substitute

1 cup unsweetened applesauce

3 tablespoons white vinegar

2 cups all-purpose flour

1 teaspoon baking soda

½ teaspoon salt

2 teaspoons pumpkin pie spice

Preheat oven to 350°F. Grease a 9-inch square cake pan with margarine or cooking spray and set aside.

Using an electric mixer at medium speed, cream sugar and margarine together until light and fluffy. Add egg whites or liquid egg substitute and mix at medium speed until creamy, scraping down the bowl before and after the addition. Add the applesauce and vinegar to the creamed mixture and mix at medium speed for 30 seconds.

Stir flour, baking soda, salt, and pumpkin pie spice together to blend well and add to the creamy mixture. Beat at medium speed for 2 minutes.

Pour the batter into the prepared pan. Bake for 50 minutes or until lightly browned and a cake tester inserted in the center comes out clean. Cool on a wire rack. Frost if desired.

NUTRITIVE VALUES PER SERVING

Number of servings 16

---

calories 164 • carbohydrate 26 grams • protein 2 grams • fat 6 grams
sodium 192 milligrams • cholesterol 0 milligrams

Low-sodium diets: Omit salt
and use salt-free margarine.

APPLESAUCE WALNUT RAISIN CAKE

You can use English walnuts in this cake, but I prefer black walnuts, which I find much more flavorful.

YIELD: ONE BUNDT CAKE

1 cup sugar

½ cup (1 stick) margarine

Dry sugar substitute equal to ½ cup sugar (optional)

2 cups unsweetened applesauce

3½ cups all-purpose flour

1 teaspoon baking powder

2 teaspoons baking soda

2 teaspoons cinnamon

½ teaspoon nutmeg

¼ cup water

½ cup chopped black or English walnuts

½ cup raisins

Preheat oven to 375°F. Grease a Bundt (fluted tube) pan with margarine or cooking spray and set aside.

Using an electric mixer at medium speed, cream sugar, margarine, and sugar substitute together until light and fluffy. Add applesauce and mix at medium speed for 1 minute, scraping down the bowl before and after the addition.

Stir flour, baking powder, baking soda, cinnamon, and nutmeg together and add, along with the water, to the creamed mixture. Mix at medium speed until creamy. Stir in the nuts and raisins.

Spread the batter evenly in the prepared pan. Bake for 1 hour and 15 minutes or until browned and firm and a cake tester inserted in the center comes out clean. Cool in the pan on a wire rack for 10 minutes. Then turn out onto the rack and cool to room temperature.

VARIATION

APPLESAUCE GRAHAM CAKE: Use 2 cups all-purpose flour and 1^1/$_3$ cups whole-wheat or graham flour instead of 3^1/$_2$ cups all-purpose flour.

NUTRITIVE VALUES PER SERVING

Number of servings 20

calories 199 • carbohydrate 33 grams • protein 3 grams • fat 6 grams
sodium 153 milligrams • cholesterol 0 milligrams

Low-sodium diets: Use salt-free margarine
and low-sodium baking powder.

BANANA DATE CAKE

YIELD: ONE 9 BY 13-INCH CAKE

½ cup (1 stick) margarine

½ cup brown sugar

½ cup sugar

½ cup egg whites or liquid egg substitute

1 teaspoon vanilla extract

2 medium bananas, sliced into ¼-inch rounds

2 cups all-purpose flour

2 tablespoons dry buttermilk

1 teaspoon baking soda

½ teaspoon salt

½ cup chopped dates

⅔ cup water, at room temperature

Preheat oven to 350°F. Grease a 9 by 13-inch cake pan with margarine or cooking spray and set aside.

Using an electric mixer at medium speed, cream margarine and sugars together until light and fluffy. Add egg whites or liquid egg substitute, vanilla, and bananas and mix at medium speed until creamy.

Stir flour, dry buttermilk, baking soda, salt, and dates together to blend and add to the creamy mixture, along with the water. Beat at medium speed until creamy again.

Spread the batter evenly in the prepared pan. Bake for 45 to 50 minutes or until lightly browned and a cake tester inserted in the center comes out clean. Cool on a rack. Frost if desired.

NUTRITIVE VALUES PER SERVING

Number of servings 20

---

calories 154 • carbohydrate 26 grams • protein 2 grams • fat 5 grams
sodium 164 milligrams • cholesterol 0 milligrams

Low-sodium diets: Omit salt
and use salt-free margarine.

DATE NUT CAKE

A sprinkling of sugar before baking gives this cake a light glaze, so it doesn't need to be frosted. It's best served warm, although it is very good at room temperature.

YIELD: ONE 9-INCH SQUARE CAKE

½ cup chopped dates

½ teaspoon baking soda

½ cup boiling water

⅓ cup (⅔ stick) margarine

⅔ cup plus 2 tablespoons sugar

¼ cup egg whites

1 teaspoon vanilla extract

1 cup all-purpose flour

¼ cup chopped English walnuts

Preheat oven to 350°F. Grease a 9-inch square cake pan with margarine or cooking spray and set aside.

Place dates in a small bowl, sprinkle with baking soda, and add boiling water. Cool to room temperature.

Using an electric mixer at medium speed, cream margarine and ⅔ cup sugar together until light and fluffy. Add egg whites and vanilla and mix at medium speed until creamy, scraping down the bowl before and after the addition.

Stir flour and nuts together and add to the creamy mixture, along with the date mixture. Mix at medium speed until creamy.

Spread the batter evenly in the prepared pan. Sprinkle the top of the batter evenly with the remaining 2 tablespoons sugar and bake for 30 minutes or until lightly browned and a cake tester inserted in the center comes out clean. Cool on a wire rack.

NUTRITIVE VALUES PER SERVING

Number of servings 16

---

calories 126 • carbohydrate 20 grams • protein 2 grams • fat 5 grams
sodium 76 milligrams • cholesterol 0 milligrams

Low-sodium diets: Use salt-free margarine.

APRICOT ALMOND CAKE

I like to use apricots and almonds the way they do in Greece and other European countries because they add a delicate flavor to this simple cake.

YIELD: ONE 9 BY 13-INCH SQUARE CAKE

1 cup plus 2 tablespoons sugar

½ cup (1 stick) margarine

½ cup egg whites or liquid egg substitute

½ teaspoon almond extract

2 cups all-purpose flour

2 tablespoons instant nonfat dry milk

1 tablespoon baking powder

⅔ cup water, at room temperature

1 cup cooked, drained, chopped dried apricots

½ cup slivered almonds

Preheat oven to 350°F. Grease a 9 by 13-inch cake pan with margarine or cooking spray and set aside.

Using an electric mixer at medium speed, cream 1 cup sugar and margarine together until light and fluffy. Add egg whites or liquid egg substitute and almond extract and mix at medium speed for 30 seconds, scraping down the bowl before and after the addition.

Stir flour, dry milk, and baking powder together to blend and add to the egg mixture, along with the water. Mix until creamy. Stir in the apricots and almonds.

Spread the batter evenly in the prepared pan. Sprinkle with the remaining 2 tablespoons sugar and bake for 40 minutes or until the cake starts to pull away from the sides of the pan and a cake tester inserted in the center comes out clean. Cool on a wire rack.

NUTRITIVE VALUES PER SERVING

Number of servings 20

---

calories 160 • carbohydrate 23 grams • protein 3 grams • fat 6 grams
sodium 116 milligrams • cholesterol 0 milligrams

Low-sodium diets: Use salt-free margarine
and low-sodium baking powder.

THE FIRST SPRING CAKE

This is the cake that lets us know that spring has finally come to Iowa. That first rhubarb is pretty and flavorful and tastes like spring because it's available only in May and June. Do not use frozen rhubarb for this cake; it retains too much moisture.

YIELD: ONE 9 BY 13-INCH CAKE

CAKE

5 cups rhubarb, cut into 1-inch pieces

1 3-ounce package strawberry-flavored gelatin

1/2 cup (1 stick) margarine

2 cups all-purpose flour

3 tablespoons instant nonfat dry milk

1 tablespoon baking powder

1/4 teaspoon salt

1/4 cup brown sugar

1 large egg white

Water, as needed

STREUSEL

1/4 cup (1/2 stick) margarine, softened

1/2 cup all-purpose flour

1 cup sugar

Preheat oven to 350°F. Grease a 9 by 13-inch cake pan with margarine or cooking spray and set aside.

Combine rhubarb and gelatin. Toss together and set aside.

Combine margarine, flour, dry milk, baking powder, salt, and brown sugar in the bowl of an electric mixer. Mix at low speed for 30 seconds to blend well. Place egg white in a measuring cup and add water to total 1 cup liquid. Add liquid to flour mixture and mix only until all of the flour is moistened.

Spread the batter evenly in the prepared pan. Using the back of a tablespoon, push the batter about 1½ inches up the sides of the pan. Spread the rhubarb and gelatin mixture evenly over the batter.

Prepare the streusel: Combine margarine, flour, and sugar and mix with a fork until crumbly. Spread evenly over the rhubarb mixture.

Bake for 50 to 60 minutes or until the cake portion springs back when touched. Cool on a wire rack. Serve warm or at room temperature.

NUTRITIVE VALUES PER SERVING

Number of servings 20

---

calories 192 • carbohydrate 30 grams • protein 2 grams • fat 7 grams
sodium 143 milligrams • cholesterol 0 milligrams

Low-sodium diets: Omit salt.
Use salt-free margarine and low-sodium baking powder.

FRUIT COCKTAIL CAKE

I've made this a small cake because it tastes best the day it is made and leftovers don't freeze well. If you want a larger cake, you can double the recipe and bake it in a 9 by 13-inch cake pan. I added oat bran to this recipe because I'm convinced it helps lower your cholesterol count. I add oat bran whenever possible if it doesn't change the flavor and texture of the cake.

YIELD: ONE 8-INCH SQUARE CAKE

¼ **cup brown sugar**

¼ **cup chopped pecans**

½ **cup all-purpose flour**

½ **cup oat bran cereal**

½ **cup sugar**

½ **teaspoon baking powder**

½ **teaspoon baking soda**

⅛ **teaspoon salt**

⅓ **cup egg whites or liquid egg substitute**

1 **cup fruit cocktail, in juice pack**

Preheat oven to 375°F. Grease an 8-inch square cake pan with margarine or cooking spray and set aside.

Combine brown sugar and nuts, mix well, and set aside.

Place flour, oat bran, sugar, baking powder, baking soda, and salt in the bowl of an electric mixer and mix at low speed to blend well. Add egg whites or liquid egg substitute, along with the fruit and juice, and mix at medium speed for 30 seconds.

Pour the batter into the prepared pan. Sprinkle the brown sugar mixture evenly over the top of the batter. Bake for 30 to 35 minutes or until the cake is lightly browned and a cake tester inserted in the center comes out clean. Serve plain or with Lemon or Orange Sauce (page 201).

NUTRITIVE VALUES PER SERVING

Number of servings 9

---

calories 146 • carbohydrate 29 grams • protein 3 grams • fat 2 grams
sodium 116 milligrams • cholesterol 0 milligrams

Low-sodium diets: Omit salt
and use low-sodium baking powder.

JAM CAKE

This dark, rich Southern cake is marvelous for holidays because it keeps so well and tastes truly festive.

YIELD: ONE BUNDT CAKE

½ cup (1 stick) margarine

1 cup sugar

1 teaspoon vanilla extract

½ cup egg whites or liquid egg substitute

2¾ cups all-purpose flour

1 teaspoon baking powder

1 teaspoon baking soda

1 teaspoon cinnamon

¼ cup dry buttermilk

1 cup water, at room temperature

1 cup Smucker's red raspberry or strawberry low-sugar spread

2 tablespoons powdered or confectioners' sugar

Preheat oven to 350°F. Grease a Bundt pan (preferably non-stick) with margarine or cooking spray. Set aside.

Using an electric mixer at medium speed, cream margarine and sugar together until light and fluffy. Add vanilla and egg whites or liquid egg substitute and beat at medium speed for 30 seconds, scraping down the bowl before and after the addition.

Stir flour, baking powder, baking soda, cinnamon, and dry buttermilk together to blend well and add to the egg mixture, along with the water. Beat at medium speed until creamy. Then add the fruit spread, mixing just to combine.

Spread the batter evenly in the prepared pan. Bake for about 1 hour or until the cake pulls away from the sides of the pan and a cake tester inserted in the center comes out clean. Cool in the pan on a wire rack for 10 to 15 minutes. Then turn out onto the rack, sprinkle with powdered sugar, and cool to room temperature.

VARIATIONS

1. JAM NUT CAKE: Add ³⁄₄ cup chopped nuts to the batter along with the fruit spread.

2. RAISIN JAM CAKE: Add ¹⁄₂ cup raisins to the batter along with the fruit spread.

NUTRITIVE VALUES PER SERVING

Number of servings 20

calories 170 • carbohydrate 28 grams • protein 3 grams • fat 5 grams
sodium 157 milligrams • cholesterol 0 milligrams

Low-sodium diets: Use salt-free margarine
and low-sodium baking powder.

PINEAPPLE CARROT CAKE

I adapted this recipe from one in a cookbook I helped write to raise money for our local library building fund. Most carrot cakes are so high in fat and sugar that I hesitate to prepare them. But this version is so good that it's hard to believe it is low in sugar and fat —and cholesterol-free.

YIELD: ONE 9 BY 13-INCH CAKE

½ cup egg whites or liquid egg substitute

1¼ cups sugar

½ cup vegetable oil

2 cups all-purpose flour

1 teaspoon baking soda

½ teaspoon salt

1 teaspoon cinnamon

1 8-ounce can crushed pineapple, in unsweetened juice

2 cups coarsely grated carrots

¾ cup Fiber One cereal

¾ cup chopped pecans

Preheat oven to 350°F. Grease a 9 by 13-inch cake pan with margarine or cooking spray and set aside.

Place egg whites or liquid egg substitute, sugar, and oil in the bowl of an electric mixer and mix at medium speed until creamy.

Stir flour, baking soda, salt, and cinnamon together to blend and add to the creamy mixture. Mix briefly. Then add the pineapple, carrots, cereal, and nuts and mix until creamy.

Pour the batter into the prepared pan. Bake for 45 minutes or until the cake pulls away from the sides of the pan and a cake tester inserted in the center comes out clean. Cool on a wire rack.

NUTRITIVE VALUES PER SERVING

Number of servings 20

---

calories 189 • carbohydrate 27 grams • protein 2 grams • fat 9 grams
sodium 109 milligrams • cholesterol 0 milligrams

Low-sodium diets: Omit salt.

PRUNE CAKE

YIELD: ONE 9 BY 13-INCH CAKE

1 cup cooked, finely chopped pitted prunes	$\frac{1}{2}$ cup egg whites or liquid egg substitute
$\frac{1}{2}$ teaspoon baking soda	2 cups all-purpose flour
$\frac{2}{3}$ cup water	$\frac{1}{4}$ cup dry buttermilk
1 cup sugar	1 teaspoon baking powder
$\frac{1}{2}$ cup (1 stick) margarine	$\frac{1}{2}$ cup chopped pecans

Preheat oven to 350°F. Grease a 9 by 13-inch cake pan with margarine or cooking spray and set aside.

Combine prunes, baking soda, and water and set aside.

Using an electric mixer at medium speed, cream sugar and margarine together until light and fluffy. Add egg whites or liquid egg substitute to the creamed mixture, scraping down the bowl before and after the addition.

Stir flour, dry buttermilk, baking powder, and pecans together to blend and add to the creamy mixture, along with the prune mixture. Mix at medium speed until creamy.

Spread the batter evenly in the prepared pan. Bake for 40 minutes or until the cake pulls away from the sides of the pan and a cake tester inserted in the center comes out clean. Cool on a wire rack. Frost if desired.

NUTRITIVE VALUES PER SERVING

Number of servings 20

---

calories 161 • carbohydrate 24 grams • protein 2 grams • fat 6 grams
sodium .103 milligrams • cholesterol 1 milligram

Low-sodium diets: Use salt-free margarine
and low-sodium baking powder.

STRAWBERRY PECAN CAKE

YIELD: ONE 9 BY 13-INCH CAKE

2 10-ounce packages frozen, sliced, sweetened strawberries

1/3 cup chopped pecans

1/3 cup brown sugar

1/2 teaspoon cinnamon

1/2 cup (1 stick) margarine

1 cup sugar

1/2 cup egg whites or liquid egg substitute, at room temperature

2 cups all-purpose flour

1/4 cup instant nonfat dry milk

2 teaspoons baking powder

1/2 teaspoon salt

2/3 cup water, at room temperature

1 tablespoon cornstarch

1 teaspoon lemon juice

Preheat oven to 350°F. Grease a 9 by 13-inch cake pan with margarine or cooking spray and set aside.

Place frozen strawberries in a colander set over a bowl. Defrost to room temperature. Reserve strawberries and juice separately.

Stir pecans, brown sugar, and cinnamon together and set aside.

Using an electric mixer at medium speed, cream margarine and sugar together until light and fluffy. Add egg whites or liquid egg substitute and mix at medium speed until creamy, scraping down the bowl before and after the addition.

Stir flour, dry milk, baking powder, and salt together to blend well and add, along with the water, to the creamy mixture. Mix at medium speed until creamy.

Spread two-thirds of the batter evenly in the prepared pan. Arrange the drained strawberries evenly over the batter and sprinkle half of the brown sugar mixture over the strawberries. Dot with the remaining batter. Then sprinkle the rest of the brown sugar mixture over the batter. Bake for 40 to 45 minutes or until lightly browned and a cake tester inserted in the center comes out clean. Cool on a wire rack.

While the cake is baking, combine the cornstarch and the reserved strawberry juice in a saucepan. Cook over medium heat, stirring constantly, until thickened and clear. Remove from heat and add lemon juice. Serve 1 tablespoon sauce over each portion of cake.

NOTE: This cake is best served warm but is also good cold. It may also be served with Whipped Topping (page 196) or Italian Meringue (page 195), along with the sauce.

NUTRITIVE VALUES PER SERVING

Number of servings 16

---

calories 231 • carbohydrate 39 grams • protein 3 grams • fat 7 grams
sodium 196 milligrams • cholesterol 0 milligrams

Low-sodium diets: Omit salt.
Use salt-free margarine and low-sodium baking powder.

EUROPEAN-STYLE CAKES

DUNDEE CAKE

JEWISH HONEY LOAF

LITHUANIAN HONEY CAKE

MADEIRA CAKE

ORANGE ALMOND CAKE

PLUM KUCHEN

POPPYSEED CAKE

RUM CAKE

I DIDN'T DISCOVER European-style cakes until I met my friend Frances Nielsen, who grew up in Luxembourg and didn't come to this country until she was eighteen. She is of Italian and Luxembourgian descent and is familiar with the foods of her homeland as well as those of Holland, Belgium, France, and Germany. She married Denny Nielsen and learned Danish cooking from his mother. A good friend instructed her in Jewish cooking and another friend, a talented pastry chef, taught her many of his professional baking skills. I was the lucky recipient of a great deal of that knowledge.

Frances introduced me to European cakes and tortes, which she loved to prepare and serve. I can't make all of them now because some of them had to have whole eggs, but we still enjoy the ones I can make with egg whites or liquid egg substitute.

Many of these cakes have a heavier texture than our light cakes but every bite is a delight. European-style cakes are almost always made with all-purpose flour instead of cake flour, and most call for lots of eggs and butter. They frequently use wine or liqueur, along with fruit, nuts, and honey; in Scotland whiskey is used as a flavoring. Many European-style cakes and tortes use chocolate, and the best recipes elevate the use of chocolate to a fine art.

If you have European cakes as part of your heritage, it is worth the effort to try to adapt them to your low-fat, low-sugar, low-cholesterol diet. Many of these old recipes use oil, which is suitable for such a diet, or butter, for which you can substitute margarine. Many recipes also call for whole eggs. You can generally substitute egg whites or liquid egg substitute for the whole eggs unless it is a recipe in which a large quantity of eggs is beaten with no other leavening. If you have a favorite recipe that has been handed down from your family, try to adapt it to suit your diet. Generally, the same substitution rates discussed in Cake Preparation (page 3) can be used for any European-style cake. However, in some cases a few tablespoons of water may need to be added to make up for the reduced fat and sugar and to give the batter the proper texture. The adapted recipe should be good but not as rich as you remember. I think it is a shame to lose our rich heritage of traditional recipes and I strongly encourage you to try your family recipes adapted for your present, more healthful diet.

Please review the seven basic rules for cake baking in Cake Preparation (page 5) before making any of the cakes in this chapter.

DUNDEE CAKE

This fruity English cake, which I fell in love with in England, is a special favorite of my friend Sandy Murray-John's English husband, Gordon. When he tasted my version of it, he said it was authentic, so I knew I had finally developed the right recipe for it.

YIELD: ONE 9 BY 5 BY 3-INCH LOAF CAKE

3/4 cup (1 1/2 sticks) margarine

3/4 cup sugar

1 cup liquid egg substitute, at room temperature

1 teaspoon lemon extract

1 teaspoon orange extract

2 1/4 cups all-purpose flour

1/2 teaspoon cinnamon

1/2 teaspoon allspice

1/2 teaspoon nutmeg

2 teaspoons baking powder

1/4 cup raisins

1/2 cup chopped candied cherries or mixed candied fruit

1/2 cup water, at room temperature

Preheat oven to 350°F. Grease a 9 by 5 by 3-inch loaf pan with margarine or cooking spray. (If it is not a non-stick pan, grease it, line it with waxed paper, and then grease again.) Set aside.

Using an electric mixer at medium speed, cream margarine and sugar together until light and fluffy. Add liquid egg substitute and flavorings and mix at medium speed until creamy, scraping down the bowl before and after the addition.

Combine flour, spices, baking powder, raisins, and chopped candied fruit (if using candied cherries instead of the candied fruit, add them after the batter is mixed). Stir to blend and then add to the creamed mixture, along with the water. Beat at medium speed until creamy.

Spread the batter evenly in the prepared pan and bake for 1 hour or until the cake is lightly browned and a cake tester inserted in the center comes out clean. Cool in the pan on a wire rack for 10 minutes. Turn out onto the rack, remove the waxed paper, and cool to room temperature. This cake is not ordinarily frosted.

NUTRITIVE VALUES PER SERVING

Number of servings 18

---

calories 186 • carbohydrate 28 grams • protein 2 grams • fat 7 grams
sodium 125 milligrams • cholesterol 0 milligrams

Low-sodium diets: Use salt-free margarine
and low-sodium baking powder.

JEWISH HONEY LOAF

This recipe is from my good friend Anita Kane of Milwaukee, Wisconsin, who has given me so many wonderful Jewish recipes.

YIELD: ONE 9 BY 5 BY 3-INCH LOAF CAKE

1 tablespoon instant coffee

1/2 cup very hot water

1/2 cup sugar

1/3 cup vegetable oil

1/3 cup egg whites or liquid egg substitute

1/2 cup honey

1 teaspoon brandy or rum flavoring

2 cups all-purpose flour

2 teaspoons baking powder

1/2 teaspoon baking soda

1/4 teaspoon salt

1/4 cup raisins

1/4 cup chopped almonds

Preheat oven to 375°F. Grease a 9 by 5 by 3-inch loaf pan with margarine or cooking spray and set aside.

Combine the instant coffee and hot water, stir to dissolve coffee, and set aside.

Place sugar, oil, egg whites or liquid egg substitute, honey, and flavoring in the bowl of an electric mixer and mix at medium speed until thick and creamy. Scrape down the bowl.

Stir flour, baking powder, baking soda, salt, raisins, and nuts together to blend well. Add to the creamy mixture, along with the dissolved coffee. Mix at medium speed for 1 minute.

Pour the batter into the prepared pan. Bake for 50 minutes or until browned and a cake tester inserted in the center comes out clean. Cool in the pan on a wire rack for 10 minutes. Then turn out onto the rack to cool to room temperature.

NUTRITIVE VALUES PER SERVING

Number of servings 20

---

calories 138 • carbohydrate 23 grams • protein 2 grams • fat 5 grams
sodium 81 milligrams • cholesterol 0 milligrams

Low-sodium diets: Omit salt.

LITHUANIAN HONEY CAKE

This is a rather dense, slightly spicy cake, which keeps well or may be frozen. I like to serve it with warm applesauce or chilled apricots.

YIELD: ONE BUNDT CAKE

1 cup liquid egg substitute,
   at room temperature

3/4 cup sugar

1/2 cup vegetable oil

1/2 cup honey, warmed

2 teaspoons vanilla extract

2 cups all-purpose flour

1/2 teaspoon baking powder

1 teaspoon baking soda

1/2 teaspoon salt

1/2 teaspoon ground cloves or
   cinnamon

Preheat oven to 350°F. Grease a Bundt (fluted tube) pan with margarine or cooking spray and set aside.

Place liquid egg substitute, sugar, and oil in the bowl of an electric mixer and mix at medium speed until creamy. Add honey (I warm it in the microwave oven for 30 seconds) and vanilla and beat at medium speed until creamy.

Stir flour, baking powder, baking soda, salt, and cloves or cinnamon together to blend well and add to the creamy mixture. Beat at medium speed for 1 minute, scraping down the bowl once.

Pour the batter into the prepared pan. Bake for 1 hour or until the cake pulls away from the sides of the pan and a cake tester inserted in the center comes out clean. Cool in the pan on a wire rack for 10 minutes. Then turn out onto the rack to cool to room temperature. This cake may be frosted, if desired, but it is generally served plain.

NUTRITIVE VALUES PER SERVING

Number of servings 18

calories 172 • carbohydrate 27 grams • protein 3 grams • fat 6 grams
sodium 146 milligrams • cholesterol 0 milligrams

Low-sodium diets: Omit salt and use
low-sodium baking powder.

MADEIRA CAKE

This English cake doesn't contain any wine. Its name comes from the wine traditionally served with it.

YIELD: ONE 9 BY 5 BY 3-INCH LOAF CAKE

¹/₂ cup (1 stick) margarine

1 cup sugar

2 teaspoons lemon extract

1 cup liquid egg substitute

1³/₄ cups all-purpose flour

1 teaspoon baking powder

¹/₄ teaspoon salt

Preheat oven to 350°F. Grease a 9 by 5 by 3-inch loaf pan with margarine or cooking spray and set aside.

Using an electric mixer at medium speed, cream margarine, sugar, and lemon extract together until light and fluffy. Add liquid egg substitute and mix at medium speed for 1 minute, scraping down the bowl before and after the addition.

Stir flour, baking powder, and salt together and add to the egg substitute mixture. Mix at medium speed for another minute.

Spread the batter evenly in the prepared pan. Bake for 1 hour or until the cake is lightly browned and a cake tester inserted in the center comes out clean. Cool in the pan on a wire rack for 10 minutes. Then turn out onto the rack to cool to room temperature. This cake is not ordinarily frosted.

NUTRITIVE VALUES PER SERVING

Number of servings 18

---

calories 138 • carbohydrate 20 grams • protein 3 grams • fat 5 grams
sodium 129 milligrams • cholesterol 0 milligrams

Low-sodium diets: Omit salt.
Use salt-free margarine and low-sodium baking powder.

ORANGE ALMOND CAKE

This Greek cake combines oranges and almonds, two common ingredients in Greek cuisine.

YIELD: ONE 9 BY 13-INCH CAKE

SYRUP

2 cups sugar

2 cups water

1/4 cup frozen orange juice
concentrate

1 teaspoon almond extract

CAKE

3/4 cup (1 1/2 sticks) margarine

1 cup sugar

2 tablespoons frozen orange
juice concentrate, thawed

1 teaspoon almond extract

1 1/2 cups uncooked instant
Cream of Wheat cereal

1 cup egg whites or liquid egg
substitute

2 cups all-purpose flour

1 teaspoon baking powder

1/2 teaspoon baking soda

1/2 teaspoon salt

3/4 cup orange juice, at room
temperature

1/2 cup slivered almonds

Preheat oven to 350°F. Grease a 9 by 13-inch cake pan with margarine or cooking spray and set aside.

Prepare the syrup: Combine sugar, water, and orange juice concentrate in a saucepan. Mix well and simmer, uncovered, for 15 minutes. Remove from heat, add almond extract, and set aside.

While the syrup is simmering, prepare the cake batter: Using an electric mixer at medium speed, cream margarine and sugar together until light and fluffy. Add orange juice concentrate and almond extract and mix at medium speed for 30 seconds. Add cereal and mix at medium speed for 30 seconds. Add egg whites or liquid egg substitute and mix at medium speed for 1 minute, scraping down the bowl before and after the addition.

Stir flour, baking powder, baking soda, and salt together and add, along with the orange juice, to the batter. Beat at medium speed until creamy. Then stir in the almonds.

Spread the batter evenly in the prepared pan. Bake for 45 minutes or until browned and a cake tester inserted in the center comes out clean.

Place the pan on a wire rack and puncture the top of the cake with a meat fork about 15 times. Pour the syrup over the cake and let it cool to room temperature.

This cake, which is fairly rich, should be cut into small pieces. I prefer 1½-inch diamonds. It can be topped with Whipped Topping (page 196) or Italian Meringue (page 195), if desired, but it is never frosted.

NOTE: This cake freezes well but it is best served slightly warm.

NUTRITIVE VALUES PER SERVING

Number of servings 30

---

calories 204 • carbohydrate 36 grams • protein 3 grams • fat 6 grams
sodium 143 milligrams • cholesterol 0 milligrams

Low-sodium diets: Omit salt.
Use salt-free margarine and low-sodium baking powder.

PLUM KUCHEN

This German cake, or Kuchen, is often served with coffee at a morning coffee break or as an afternoon snack. Other kinds of fruit, such as apples or peaches, may be used in place of the plums.

YIELD: ONE 12 BY 18-INCH CAKE

¹/₂ cup hot water

¹/₂ cup plus 2 tablespoons sugar

2 tablespoons instant nonfat dry milk

1 packet (2¹/₄ teaspoons) active dry yeast

2 cups all-purpose flour

¹/₄ cup egg whites or liquid egg substitute

¹/₂ teaspoon salt

¹/₂ teaspoon lemon extract

¹/₂ teaspoon ground cardamom

¹/₄ cup plus 2 tablespoons (³/₄ stick) margarine

2¹/₂ pounds fresh prune plums

1 tablespoon cornstarch

¹/₂ teaspoon cinnamon

Combine hot water, 2 tablespoons sugar, and dry milk and stir to dissolve sugar. Cool to 110° to 115°F. Add yeast, mix lightly, and let stand for 10 minutes.

Add flour, egg whites or liquid egg substitute, salt, lemon extract, cardamom, and $\frac{1}{4}$ cup margarine to the yeast mixture. Using an electric mixer with a dough hook, mix at low speed 3 to 4 minutes or until the dough forms a ball. Turn the dough out onto a lightly floured working surface and knead lightly. Round into a ball and place in a bowl that has been greased with margarine. Turn the ball over to coat the top with margarine. Cover and let stand until doubled in volume.

While the dough is rising, wash, pit, and quarter the plums and set aside.

Stir the remaining $\frac{1}{2}$ cup sugar, cornstarch, and cinnamon together to blend and set aside.

When the dough has risen, turn it out on a floured working surface and knead lightly. Form into a ball, cover with a cloth, and let stand for 10 minutes. Roll dough into a 12 by 18-inch oblong and place it on a greased 12 by 18-inch cookie sheet with raised sides. Over very low heat or in the microwave, melt the remaining 2 tablespoons margarine. While the margarine is melting, place the plums, cut side down, in even rows on the dough, leaving a $\frac{1}{2}$-inch border without any fruit. Sprinkle the sugar mixture evenly over the fruit. Then drizzle the melted margarine over the sugar mixture. Cover with waxed paper, then a cloth, and let the kuchen rise in a warm place for about 30 minutes.

Bake in a preheated 400°F oven for 20 to 30 minutes or until the fruit is soft and the crust is lightly browned. Serve warm or at room temperature.

NUTRITIVE VALUES PER SERVING
Number of servings 20

---

calories 146 • carbohydrate 27 grams • protein 3 grams • fat 3 grams
sodium 101 milligrams • cholesterol 0 milligrams

Low-sodium diets: Omit salt
and use salt-free margarine.

POPPYSEED CAKE

I got this recipe from a friend of mine when we lived in Chicago, a city with a large Polish population. If your supermarkets don't carry Solo Poppy Filling, they can probably order it for you. The manufacturer assures me that it is available nationally.

YIELD: ONE BUNDT CAKE

³/₄ cup egg whites or liquid egg substitute

¹/₂ cup vegetable oil

1 cup sugar

1 12¹/₂-ounce can Solo Poppy Filling

3 cups all-purpose flour

1¹/₂ teaspoons baking soda

1 12-ounce can evaporated skim milk

Preheat oven to 375°F. Grease a Bundt (fluted tube) pan with margarine or cooking spray and set aside.

Combine egg whites or liquid egg substitute, oil, and sugar in the bowl of an electric mixer and mix at medium speed until creamy. Add poppy filling and mix at medium speed for another minute. Stir flour and baking soda together to blend and add to poppy mixture, along with the milk. Mix at medium speed for 2 minutes.

Pour the batter into the prepared pan. Bake for 1 hour or until the cake pulls away from the sides of the pan and a cake tester inserted in the center comes out clean. Cool on a wire rack for 10 minutes. Then turn out onto the rack and cool to room temperature. This cake is generally served without frosting but can be frosted with Vanilla Powdered Sugar Frosting (page 192).

NUTRITIVE VALUES PER SERVING

Number of servings 20

---

calories 231 • carbohydrate 36 grams • protein 5 grams • fat 8 grams
sodium 383 milligrams • cholesterol 1 milligram

Low-sodium diets: Use at your own discretion.

RUM CAKE

There are several types of rum cake, but this one, which is based on a French savarin cake, is my favorite.

YIELD: ONE 10-INCH TUBE CAKE, BUNDT CAKE, OR 10- TO 12-INCH RING CAKE

CAKE

1/4 cup instant nonfat dry milk

1/4 cup sugar

1 cup hot water

1 packet (2 1/4 teaspoons) quick-rising active dry yeast

2 3/4 cups bread flour

1 teaspoon salt

1 teaspoon vanilla extract

1/4 cup (1/2 stick) margarine, softened

1/2 cup egg whites or liquid egg substitute, at room temperature

RUM SAUCE

1 cup sugar

1/2 cup light corn syrup

1/2 cup water

1/4 cup rum

Place dry milk and sugar in the bowl of an electric mixer. Add the hot water and mix to dissolve the sugar. Cool to 110° to 115°F. Add the yeast, mix lightly, and let stand about 10 minutes or until bubbly. Add 1½ cups of the flour and mix at medium speed, using a dough hook, for 4 minutes. Add salt, vanilla, margarine, egg whites or liquid egg substitute, and remaining 1¼ cups flour and mix again for 4 minutes.

Spread the batter evenly in a greased 10-inch tube, Bundt (fluted tube), or 10- to 12-inch ring pan. Cover with a cloth and let rise at room temperature until doubled in volume.

Bake in a preheated 350°F oven for 50 to 60 minutes or until golden brown.

While the cake is baking, prepare the Rum Sauce: Combine sugar, corn syrup, and water in a saucepan. Stir over low heat until the sugar is dissolved. Then simmer, uncovered, for 5 minutes. Remove the syrup from heat, add the rum, and let stand at room temperature until needed.

When the cake is done, let it cool in the pan for 5 minutes. Then turn out onto a wire rack and puncture about 15 holes in the bottom of the cake with a skewer or meat fork. Pour the syrup into the bottom of the cake pan, return the cake to the pan, and let it stand at room temperature for about 30 minutes to absorb the syrup.

NOTE: This cake may be served warm or at room temperature. It is very good when garnished with Whipped Topping (page 196) or Custard Sauce (page 200).

NUTRITIVE VALUES PER SERVING

Number of servings 20

---

calories 165 • carbohydrate 32 grams • protein 3 grams • fat 2 grams
sodium 339 milligrams • cholesterol 0 milligrams

Low-sodium diets: Omit salt
and use salt-free margarine.

LIGHT

CAKES

ANGEL FOOD CAKE

CHOCOLATE ANGEL FOOD CAKE

CHOCOLATE PEPPERMINT ANGEL FOOD CAKE

CHOCOLATE RUM ANGEL FOOD CAKE

BURNT SUGAR CAKE

CARAMEL CAKE

CARAMEL PECAN CAKE

MAPLE SYRUP CAKE

MAPLE BIRTHDAY CAKE

PEANUT BUTTER CRUMB CAKE

WHITE CAKE

ALMOND CAKE

BLACK WALNUT CAKE

PRETTY PINK PEPPERMINT CAKE

MOIST WHITE CAKE

———

WHEN I REFER TO "light cakes," I am referring to cakes that resemble those made from a cake mix, most of which have a light, airy texture with a smooth crumb. They are delicious and I'm sure we all enjoy them whether they are made from scratch or from a mix.

I don't disapprove of cakes made from mixes. In fact, there are mixes that can be adapted for a low-cholesterol diet. You probably won't find mixes with a reduced sugar content, unless they are advertised as diabetic cake mixes, but you can find some that let you control the amount of fat you add to them. The trick to using cake mixes is to buy those that direct you to add the fat (preferably oil), whole eggs, or milk or water. This way you can substitute egg whites or liquid egg substitute and reconstituted instant nonfat dry milk for the forbidden ingredients. However, you must read the ingredient list very carefully because some cake mixes contain hydrogenated animal fat and still direct you to add oil to the mix. Until manufacturers see fit to provide cake mixes (other than angel food mixes) suitable for a low-cholesterol diet, I urge you to prepare the recipes in this chapter, which I am sure are suitable for your diet.

If you use a cake mix, follow the directions exactly, substituting the ingredients necessary for a low-cholesterol diet. A lot of time and effort has gone into those directions. Most manufacturers have a staff of dietitians, home economists, and/or food technologists who have worked hard to perfect those directions so you will get the best results. After you have prepared a cake from a mix, you may want to experiment and create new and interesting cakes, but don't do it the first time. My friend Mary Boineau of Tampa, Florida, does marvelous things with cake mixes, but she follows the directions whenever she uses a mix for the first time.

The recipes in this chapter use less sugar and fat than cake mixes. I think you'll find that they add interest and variety to your low-fat, low-sugar, low-cholesterol diet.

Please review the seven basic rules for cake baking in Cake Preparation (page 5) before making any of the cakes in this chapter.

ANGEL FOOD CAKE

Commercial angel food cake mixes are well and good, but this is so much better. I make this cake for special occasions.

YIELD: ONE 10-INCH TUBE CAKE

1 cup plus 2 tablespoons cake flour

1 cup plus 2 tablespoons powdered or confectioners' sugar

1¼ cups egg whites

1½ teaspoons cream of tartar

1 teaspoon vanilla extract

1 teaspoon almond extract

1 cup plus 2 tablespoons sugar

Preheat oven to 350°F.

Combine cake flour and powdered sugar and stir vigorously for 1 minute. (This will aerate the mixture so it will not require sifting.) Set aside.

Using an electric mixer with a whip attachment, beat the egg whites at high speed until frothy. With the mixer running on low, add cream of tartar and flavorings. Then gradually add the sugar and continue beating at high speed until stiff. Reduce mixer speed to low and gradually add the flour mixture, beating just until incorporated.

Spread the batter evenly in a clean, ungreased 10-inch tube pan. Draw a knife through the batter to release air bubbles, which could cause holes to form in the cake. Bake for 1 hour or until the cake is lightly browned and begins to pull away from the sides of the pan. Remove from the oven, invert the pan, and allow the cake to cool completely before removing it from the pan. Frost lightly if desired.

NUTRITIVE VALUES PER SERVING

Number of servings 18

---

calories 105 • carbohydrate 24 grams • protein 2 grams • fat 0 grams
sodium 28 milligrams • cholesterol 0 milligrams

Low-sodium diets: Recipe may be used as written.

CHOCOLATE ANGEL FOOD CAKE

YIELD: ONE 10-INCH TUBE CAKE

$^3/_4$ cup cake flour

$^1/_4$ cup cocoa

1$^1/_4$ cups egg whites, at room
  temperature

1 teaspoon cream of tartar

1 teaspoon vanilla extract

1$^1/_4$ cups sugar

Preheat oven to 325°F.

Place cake flour and cocoa in a bowl and stir vigorously with a spoon. (This will aerate the mixture so it will not require sifting.) Set aside.

Using an electric mixer with a whip attachment, beat egg whites at high speed until frothy. Add the cream of tartar and vanilla and continue to beat at high speed, adding the sugar gradually, until the egg white mixture is glossy and holds a peak. Reduce mixer speed to low and add the flour and cocoa mixture gradually. Continue mixing just to combine.

Spread the batter evenly in an ungreased 10-inch tube pan. Bake 1 hour or until the cake starts to pull away from the sides of the pan. Remove from the oven, invert pan, and allow the cake to cool completely before removing it from the pan.

VARIATIONS

1. CHOCOLATE PEPPERMINT ANGEL FOOD CAKE: Omit the vanilla and add 1 teaspoon peppermint flavoring.

2. CHOCOLATE RUM ANGEL FOOD CAKE: Add 1 teaspoon rum flavoring along with the vanilla.

NUTRITIVE VALUES PER SERVING
Number of servings 16

calories 89 • carbohydrate 20 grams • protein 2 grams • fat 0 grams
sodium 32 milligrams • cholesterol 0 milligrams

Low-sodium diets: Recipe may be used as written.

BURNT SUGAR CAKE

This cake seems to have lost the popularity it enjoyed around the turn of the century, which is a shame because it is a very good cake. I'm sure you will enjoy it when you try it.

YIELD: TWO 9-INCH LAYERS

CAKE

1 cup sugar, divided

1 cup boiling water

1/2 cup (1 stick) margarine

1 teaspoon vanilla extract

1/4 cup egg whites

2 1/2 cups cake flour

1 tablespoon baking powder

1/4 teaspoon salt

1/4 cup instant nonfat dry milk

BURNT SUGAR FROSTING

1 cup sugar

3/4 cup boiling water

1/4 cup egg whites

1/4 teaspoon cream of tartar

1/4 teaspoon salt

Preheat oven to 350°F. Grease two 9-inch layer cake pans with margarine or cooking spray. Line with waxed paper circles and set aside.

In a small heavy saucepan, melt 1/2 cup sugar, stirring constantly with a wooden spoon until the sugar is a rich, caramel color. Remove the pan from the heat and add the boiling water. Return to the heat and continue to cook, stirring, until the caramelized sugar and water are mixed and there are no lumps of caramelized sugar left in the pan. Set aside to cool to room temperature.

Using an electric mixer at medium speed, cream margarine, remaining 1/2 cup sugar, and vanilla together until light and fluffy. Add egg whites to the creamy mixture and mix at medium speed until smooth, scraping down the bowl before and after the addition.

Stir flour, baking powder, salt, and dry milk together to blend and then add, along with the caramelized sugar mixture, to the egg mixture. Mix at medium speed until smooth.

Pour half of the batter into each of the prepared pans. Bake for 30 minutes or until the layers pull away from the sides of the pans and a cake tester inserted in the center of each layer comes out clean. Cool in the pans for 10 minutes. Then turn out onto a wire rack, remove waxed paper, and cool to room temperature.

To prepare the frosting: Melt ¾ cup sugar in a small heavy saucepan, stirring constantly with a wooden spoon until the sugar is a rich caramel color. Remove the pan from heat and add the boiling water. Return to low heat and continue to cook, stirring until the sugar and water are thoroughly mixed. Cook the caramelized syrup over low heat, stirring occasionally, until it registers 238°F on a candy thermometer. Remove from heat.

Using an electric mixer with a whip attachment, beat the egg whites, cream of tartar, and salt at high speed until foamy. Gradually add the remaining ¼ cup sugar, while continuing to beat at high speed, until the meringue holds a peak. Pour the hot syrup into the meringue in a very thin stream and continue to beat until the frosting is cool and stiff. Frost the cake only when completely cooled.

NOTE: This frosting does not freeze well.

NUTRITIVE VALUES PER SERVING WITH FROSTING
Number of servings 16

---

calories 209 • carbohydrate 37 grams • protein 2 grams • fat 6 grams
sodium 214 milligrams • cholesterol 0 milligrams

Low-sodium diets: Omit salt.
Use salt-free margarine and low-sodium baking powder.

NUTRITIVE VALUES PER SERVING WITHOUT FROSTING

Number of servings 16

---

calories 159 • carbohydrate 25 grams • protein 2 grams • fat 6 grams
sodium 174 milligrams • cholesterol 0 milligrams

Low-sodium diets: Omit salt.
Use salt-free margarine and low-sodium baking powder.

CARAMEL CAKE

YIELD: ONE 9-INCH SQUARE CAKE

1 cup brown sugar

$^1/_2$ cup (1 stick) margarine

$^1/_4$ cup egg whites or liquid egg
substitute

1 teaspoon caramel flavoring

2 cups all-purpose flour

2 tablespoons instant nonfat
dry milk

2 teaspoons baking powder

$^1/_4$ teaspoon salt

1 cup water, at room
temperature

Preheat oven to 350°F. Grease a 9-inch square cake pan with margarine
or cooking spray and set aside.

Using an electric mixer at medium speed, cream brown sugar and margarine together until light and fluffy. Add egg whites or liquid egg substitute
and flavoring and mix at medium speed until creamy, scraping down the
bowl before and after the addition.

Stir flour, dry milk, baking powder, and salt together and add to the
creamy mixture, along with the water. Mix at medium speed until creamy.

Spread the batter evenly in the prepared pan. Bake for 40 minutes or until the cake pulls away from the sides of the pan and a cake tester inserted in the center comes out clean. Cool on a wire rack. Frost if desired.

VARIATION

CARAMEL PECAN CAKE: Add ½ cup chopped pecans along with the flour and water.

NUTRITIVE VALUES PER SERVING

Number of servings 16

---

calories 163 • carbohydrate 26 grams • protein 2 grams • fat 6 grams
sodium 156 milligrams • cholesterol 0 milligrams

Low-sodium diets: Omit salt.
Use salt-free margarine and low-sodium baking powder.

MAPLE SYRUP CAKE

I developed this cake as a surprise for a friend who is very fond of maple syrup. I frosted it with White Mountain Frosting (page 188) for her birthday and she loved it.

YIELD: ONE 9 BY 13-INCH CAKE OR TWO
9-INCH LAYERS

½ cup brown sugar

1 cup maple syrup

¾ cup (1½ sticks) margarine, softened

¼ cup egg whites or liquid egg substitute

2½ cups all-purpose flour

1 tablespoon baking powder

¼ teaspoon salt

¼ cup instant nonfat dry milk

½ cup water, at room temperature

Preheat oven to 350°F. Grease a 9 by 13-inch cake pan with margarine or cooking spray and set aside.

Using an electric mixer at medium speed, cream brown sugar, syrup, and margarine together until creamy and smooth. Add egg whites or liquid egg substitute and beat at medium speed until creamy again, scraping down the bowl before and after the addition.

Stir flour, baking powder, salt, and dry milk together to blend and add, along with the water, to the egg mixture. Beat at medium speed until creamy.

Spread the batter evenly in the prepared pan. Bake for 35 minutes or until the cake pulls away from the sides of the pan and a cake tester inserted in the center comes out clean. Cool on a wire rack.

NOTE: For a more intense maple flavor, add 1 teaspoon maple flavoring.

VARIATION

MAPLE BIRTHDAY CAKE: Spread half of the batter in each of two greased, waxed paper–lined 9-inch layer cake pans. Bake for about 30 minutes or until the cake pulls away from the sides of the pan and a cake tester inserted in the center comes out clean. Cool in the pan on a wire rack for 10 minutes. Then turn out onto the rack, remove the waxed paper, and cool to room temperature. Frost with Maple Syrup Frosting (page 187) or White Mountain Frosting (page 188) and decorate as desired.

NUTRITIVE VALUES PER SERVING

Number of servings 24

---

calories 153 • carbohydrate 24 grams • protein 2 grams • fat 6 grams
sodium 148 milligrams • cholesterol 0 milligrams

Low-sodium diets: Omit salt.
Use salt-free margarine and low-sodium baking powder.

PEANUT BUTTER CRUMB CAKE

Anyone who likes peanut butter will enjoy this cake. I make it with chunky peanut butter but smooth peanut butter works just as well.

YIELD: ONE 9 BY 13-INCH CAKE

1 cup brown sugar

2¼ cups all-purpose flour

½ cup (1 stick) margarine

¾ cup chunky peanut butter

2 teaspoons baking powder

2 tablespoons instant nonfat
   dry milk

½ cup egg whites or liquid egg
   substitute

½ cup water

1 teaspoon vanilla extract

Preheat oven to 350°F. Grease a 9 by 13-inch cake pan with margarine or cooking spray and set aside.

Place brown sugar, flour, margarine, and peanut butter in the bowl of an electric mixer and mix at low speed until well blended. Reserve ⅔ cup of the mixture. Add baking powder and dry milk to the mixture left in the bowl and mix at low speed to blend. Combine egg whites or liquid egg substitute, water, and vanilla and mix lightly. Add to the peanut butter mixture in the bowl and mix at medium speed until creamy.

Spread the batter evenly in the prepared pan. Spread the reserved peanut butter mixture over the batter and bake for 35 minutes or until the cake pulls away from the sides of the pan and a cake tester inserted in the center comes out clean. Cool on a wire rack. Serve with Powdered Sugar Glaze (page 193) if desired.

NUTRITIVE VALUES PER SERVING

Number of servings 24

---

calories 162 • carbohydrate 20 grams • protein 4 grams • fat 8 grams
sodium 124 milligrams • cholesterol 0 milligrams

Low-sodium diets: Use salt-free margarine,
low-sodium baking powder,
and salt-free peanut butter, if available.

WHITE CAKE

*I make the Black Walnut Cake variation of this recipe for family potluck dinners
and it is a hit every time.*

YIELD: TWO 9-INCH LAYERS

½ cup (1 stick) margarine

1¼ cups sugar

1 teaspoon vanilla extract

1 teaspoon almond extract
(optional)

½ cup egg whites, at room
temperature

2¼ cups all-purpose flour

¼ teaspoon salt

2 teaspoons baking powder

¼ cup instant nonfat dry milk

1 cup water, at room
temperature

Preheat oven to 375°F. Grease two 9-inch layer cake pans with margarine
or cooking spray. Line with waxed paper circles and set aside.

Using an electric mixer at medium speed, cream margarine and sugar together until light and fluffy. Add vanilla and almond extracts, then egg whites, 1/4 cup at a time, scraping down the bowl and beating well after each addition.

Stir flour, salt, baking powder, and dry milk together to blend well and add to the egg mixture, along with the water. Beat only until smooth.

Pour half of the batter into each of the prepared pans. Bake for 30 minutes or until the cake layers are lightly browned and pull away from the sides of the pans. Cool in the pans on a wire rack for 10 minutes. Then turn out onto the rack, remove waxed paper, and cool to room temperature. Frost as desired.

VARIATIONS

1. ALMOND CAKE: Use almond flavoring and add 3/4 cups slivered almonds along with the flour mixture.

2. BLACK WALNUT CAKE: Omit almond flavoring and add 3/4 cup chopped black walnuts and 1 teaspoon black walnut flavoring.

3. PRETTY PINK PEPPERMINT CAKE: Omit almond flavoring and add 2 or 3 drops of red food coloring and 1 teaspoon peppermint flavoring.

NUTRITIVE VALUES PER SERVING

Number of servings 16

calories 182 • carbohydrate 30 grams • protein 3 grams • fat 6 grams
sodium 160 milligrams • cholesterol 0 milligrams

Low-sodium diets: Omit salt.
Use salt-free margarine and low-sodium baking powder.

MOIST WHITE CAKE

This moist, fine-grained cake is just the thing for anyone who prefers to bake with vegetable oil. The cake can also be made in three 8-inch layers.

YIELD: TWO 9-INCH LAYERS

2 cups cake flour

1 1/2 cups sugar

1/4 cup instant nonfat dry milk

2 teaspoons baking powder

1 teaspoon baking soda

1/2 teaspoon salt

1 cup water, at room temperature

1/2 cup egg whites

2/3 cup vegetable oil

2 teaspoons vanilla extract

Preheat oven to 350°F. Grease two 9-inch layer cake pans with margarine or cooking spray. Line with waxed paper circles and set aside.

Place cake flour, sugar, dry milk, baking powder, baking soda, and salt in the bowl of an electric mixer and mix at low speed for 30 seconds to blend well. Stir water, egg whites, oil, and vanilla together with a fork and add to the flour mixture. Mix at medium speed for 1 to 2 minutes or until creamy and smooth.

Pour half of the batter into each of the prepared pans. Bake for 25 to 30 minutes or until the layers are lightly browned and pull away from the sides of the pans. Cool in the pans on a wire rack for 10 minutes. Then turn out onto the rack, remove waxed paper, and cool to room temperature. Frost as desired.

NUTRITIVE VALUES PER SERVING

Number of servings 16

---

calories 226 • carbohydrate 34 grams • protein 2 grams • fat 9 grams
sodium 178 milligrams • cholesterol 0 milligrams

Low-sodium diets: Omit salt
and use low-sodium baking powder.

SPICE

CAKES

CARDAMOM CAKE

GINGERBREAD

GINGER SPONGE CAKE

VERA'S GINGER CAKE

MOLASSES SPICE CAKE

OATMEAL SPICE CAKE

PUMPKIN SPICE CAKE

PUMPKIN PECAN SPICE CAKE

PUMPKIN DATE SPICE CAKE

PUMPKIN RAISIN SPICE CAKE

RAISIN SPICE CAKE

SUPREME SPICE CAKE

TOMATO SPICE CAKE

IT'S HARD TO believe that wars were fought, fortunes were won, and lives were lost over the spices we take for granted in our spice racks. In the Middle Ages, when spices became popular in the western world, only wealthy families could afford to use spices for flavoring their food. The lady of the manor kept them in locked cabinets, since some of them were literally worth their weight in gold.

Now that spices are freely available, we use them lavishly. Most people have childhood memories of comfort foods seasoned with a certain spice, which they recall when they taste or smell that favorite spice again. I have a friend who loves one of my cookies. We couldn't understand why she was so fond of that particular cookie until she remembered that her Scandinavian grandmother had also used that same spice, cardamom, in her cookies. I love the smell of cinnamon — my grandmother and mother's favorite spice — because it evokes happy memories of cinnamon rolls and apple pie. I'm sure you also have favorite spices, and if you think your favorite spice would enhance a recipe in this book, feel free to substitute it for the spice I have used. It won't change the nutritive value of the recipes. There are also some combinations of spices, such as that in Supreme Spice Cake (page 101), that you may want to use in other recipes. If you have your own favorite mixture of spices, you can combine them in the right proportions and keep them in a glass or metal container to use when you need them.

Spices should be kept in an airtight glass or metal container away from extreme heat and direct sunlight. I like to buy my spices in small quantities (so they get used up quickly), except for cinnamon, which I use frequently. Old spices that have lost their pungency should be discarded.

Spice cakes have been around for a long time and it looks as though they will continue to be popular for years to come. They are tasty, they add an interesting note to your meals or snacks, and they are loved by almost everyone.

Please review the seven basic rules for cake baking in Cake Preparation (page 5) before making any of the cakes in this chapter.

CARDAMOM CAKE

The hint of cardamom in this cake appeals to my Scandinavian friends because it reminds them of the cakes and cookies they enjoyed as children.

YIELD: ONE 9-INCH SQUARE CAKE

½ cup (1 stick) margarine

1 cup sugar

½ cup egg whites or liquid egg substitute

1 teaspoon lemon extract

2 cups cake flour

¼ cup dry buttermilk

1 teaspoon cardamom

1 teaspoon baking soda

1 cup water, at room temperature

Preheat oven to 350°F. Grease a 9-inch square cake pan with margarine or cooking spray and set aside.

Using an electric mixer at medium speed, cream margarine and sugar together until light and fluffy. Add egg whites or liquid egg substitute and lemon extract and mix at medium speed until creamy, scraping down the bowl before and after the addition.

Stir flour, dry buttermilk, cardamom, and baking soda together to blend well and then add, along with the water, to the creamy mixture. Mix at medium speed until creamy.

Spread the batter evenly in the prepared pan. Bake for 35 minutes or until the cake pulls away from the sides of the pan and a cake tester inserted in the center comes out clean. Cool on a wire rack.

NUTRITIVE VALUES PER SERVING

Number of servings 16

---

calories 154 • carbohydrate 23 grams • protein 2 grams • fat 6 grams
sodium 141 milligrams • cholesterol 1 milligram

Low-sodium diets: Use salt-free margarine.

GINGERBREAD

Gingerbread is delicious plain, but two tablespoons of powdered sugar will dress it up for a special occasion and add less than one gram carbohydrate per serving and no fat or cholesterol.

YIELD: ONE 9-INCH SQUARE CAKE

⅓ cup (⅔ stick) margarine	1 teaspoon baking soda
½ cup molasses	1 teaspoon cinnamon
½ cup sugar	1 teaspoon ground ginger
¼ cup egg whites or liquid egg substitute	¼ teaspoon salt
2 cups all-purpose flour	1 cup water, at room temperature
1 teaspoon baking powder	

Preheat oven to 375°F. Grease a 9-inch square cake pan with margarine or cooking spray and set aside.

Using an electric mixer at medium speed, cream margarine, molasses, and sugar together until light and fluffy. Add egg whites or liquid egg substitute and beat at medium speed until creamy, scraping down the bowl before and after the addition.

Stir flour, baking powder, baking soda, cinnamon, ginger, and salt together to blend and add to the egg mixture, along with the water. Beat at medium speed until creamy.

Pour the batter into the prepared pan. Bake for 40 minutes or until the gingerbread pulls away from the sides of the pan and a cake tester inserted in the center comes out clean. Cool on a wire rack and serve warm or at room temperature.

NUTRITIVE VALUES PER SERVING

Number of servings 16

---

calories 137 • carbohydrate 24 grams • protein 2 grams • fat 4 grams
sodium 165 milligrams • cholesterol 0 milligrams

Low-sodium diets: Omit salt.
Use salt-free margarine and low-sodium baking powder.

GINGER SPONGE CAKE

I found this recipe in a 1910 cookbook published by the young people's group of our church. Because of the name, I expected a cake with a different texture. But what I got was simply an excellent ginger cake. I use a plain vanilla frosting on it so as not to overpower the spices in the cake.

YIELD: ONE 9-INCH SQUARE CAKE

½ cup (1 stick) margarine

1 cup boiling water

⅓ cup sugar

⅓ cup molasses

2¼ cups all-purpose flour

2 teaspoons baking soda

1 teaspoon ground ginger

½ teaspoon ground cloves

½ teaspoon cinnamon

⅓ cup egg whites or liquid egg substitute

Preheat oven to 350°F. Grease a 9-inch square cake pan with margarine or cooking spray and set aside.

Cut the margarine into quarters and place in the bowl of an electric mixer. Add the boiling water and mix at low speed to melt margarine. Add sugar and molasses, mix lightly, and cool to room temperature.

Stir flour, baking soda, and spices together to blend well and add, along with the egg whites or liquid egg substitute, to the molasses mixture. Mix at medium speed for 1 minute.

Pour the batter into the prepared pan. Bake for 30 minutes or until the cake starts to pull away from the sides of the pan and a cake tester inserted in the center comes out clean. Cool on a wire rack. Frost if desired.

NUTRITIVE VALUES PER SERVING

Number of servings 16

---

calories 147 • carbohydrate 21 grams • protein 2 grams • fat 6 grams
sodium 185 milligrams • cholesterol 0 milligrams

Low-sodium diets: Use salt-free margarine.

VERA'S GINGER CAKE

My friends who like ginger really enjoy this cake, which was a specialty of my good friend Vera Wilson.

YIELD: ONE 9-INCH SQUARE CAKE

½ cup liquid egg substitute

½ cup molasses

½ cup sugar

½ cup (1 stick) margarine, softened

½ cup hot water

2 cups all-purpose flour

1 teaspoon ground ginger

1 teaspoon baking soda

1 tablespoon finely chopped fresh gingerroot or crystallized ginger

Preheat oven to 350°F. Grease a 9-inch square cake pan with margarine or cooking spray and set aside.

Combine liquid egg substitute, molasses, and sugar in the bowl of an electric mixer, and beat at medium speed for 1 minute. Add margarine and water and beat at medium speed for another minute, scraping down the bowl before and after the addition.

Stir flour, ground ginger, and baking soda together to blend and add to the creamy mixture. Mix at medium speed for 1 minute. Stir in the fresh or crystallized ginger.

Pour the batter into the prepared pan. Bake for 30 to 35 minutes or until the cake pulls away from the sides of the pan and a cake tester inserted in the center comes out clean. Cool on a wire rack.

NUTRITIVE VALUES PER SERVING

Number of servings 16

calories 156 • carbohydrate 24 grams • protein 3 grams • fat 6 grams
sodium 87 milligrams • cholesterol 0 milligrams

Low-sodium diets: Use salt-free margarine.

MOLASSES SPICE CAKE

I am very sentimental about this cake. I made it for my husband on his birthday not long before we were married and it became one of our favorites. Back then I frosted it with a rich caramel frosting, but in later years I spread jelly between the layers and glazed it with Powdered Sugar Glaze (page 193).

YIELD: TWO 9-INCH LAYERS

½ cup (1 stick) margarine

¾ cup sugar

⅓ cup egg whites or liquid egg substitute, at room temperature

⅓ cup light molasses

2½ cups all-purpose flour

¼ cup instant nonfat dry milk

2½ teaspoons baking powder

1 teaspoon cinnamon

¼ teaspoon salt

¾ cup water, at room temperature

Preheat oven to 350°F. Grease two 9-inch layer cake pans with margarine or cooking spray and set aside.

Using an electric mixer at medium speed, cream margarine and sugar together until light and fluffy. Add egg whites or liquid egg substitute and molasses and mix at medium speed until creamy, scraping down the bowl before and after the addition.

Stir flour, dry milk, baking powder, cinnamon, and salt together to blend well and add to the creamy mixture, along with the water. Mix at medium speed until creamy.

Spread half of the batter in each of the prepared pans. Bake for 30 to 35 minutes or until the layers pull away from the sides of the pans and a cake tester inserted in the center comes out clean. Cool on a wire rack. Frost if desired.

NUTRITIVE VALUES PER SERVING

Number of servings 16

---

calories 179 • carbohydrate 29 grams • protein 3 grams • fat 6 grams
sodium 173 milligrams • cholesterol 0 milligrams

Low-sodium diets: Omit salt.
Use salt-free margarine and low-sodium baking powder.

OATMEAL SPICE CAKE

YIELD: ONE 9 BY 13-INCH CAKE

½ cup (1 stick) margarine

1 cup sugar

¼ cup egg whites or liquid egg
   substitute

1 teaspoon vanilla extract

1½ cups unsweetened
   applesauce

2 cups all-purpose flour

½ cup rolled oats

1½ teaspoons cinnamon

2 teaspoons baking soda

½ cup raisins

Preheat oven to 350°F. Grease a 9 by 13-inch cake pan with margarine or cooking spray and set aside.

Using an electric mixer at medium speed, cream margarine and sugar together until light and fluffy. Add egg whites or liquid egg substitute and vanilla and mix at medium speed until creamy, scraping down the bowl before and after the addition. Add the applesauce and mix at medium speed for 30 seconds.

Stir flour, oatmeal, cinnamon, baking soda, and raisins together to blend and add to the applesauce mixture. Mix at medium speed for 1 minute.

Spread the batter evenly in the prepared pan. Bake for 35 to 40 minutes or until the cake pulls away from the sides of the pan and the cake tester inserted in the center comes out clean. Cool on a wire rack. Frost if desired.

NUTRITIVE VALUES PER SERVING

Number of servings 20

calories 152 • carbohydrate 26 grams • protein 2 grams • fat 5 grams
sodium 141 milligrams • cholesterol 0 milligrams

Low-sodium diets: Use salt-free margarine.

PUMPKIN SPICE CAKE

This pretty cake is one I usually frost with Creamy Lemon Frosting or Creamy Orange Frosting (page 186). I also like to decorate it in the fall with candy corns or Halloween candies shaped like pumpkins and witches.

*YIELD: TWO 9-INCH LAYERS OR ONE
9 BY 13-INCH CAKE*

½ cup (1 stick) margarine

½ cup sugar

½ cup brown sugar

½ cup egg whites or liquid egg substitute

1 teaspoon vanilla extract

1 cup cooked, mashed pumpkin or pumpkin puree

2²/₃ cups cake flour

1 tablespoon baking powder

1 teaspoon baking soda

1½ teaspoons pumpkin pie spice

½ cup water, at room temperature

Preheat oven to 350°F. Grease two 9-inch layer cake pans with margarine or cooking spray. Line with waxed paper circles and set aside.

Using an electric mixer at medium speed, cream margarine and sugars together until light and fluffy. Add egg whites or liquid egg substitute, vanilla, and pumpkin and mix at medium speed until creamy, scraping down the bowl before and after the addition.

Stir cake flour, baking powder, baking soda, and pumpkin pie spice together to blend and add to the creamy mixture, along with the water. Mix at medium speed until creamy.

Pour half of the batter into each of the prepared pans. Bake for 35 minutes or until the layers pull away from the sides of the pans and a cake tester inserted in the center of each layer comes out clean. Cool in the pans on a wire rack for 10 minutes. Then turn out onto the rack, remove the waxed paper, and cool to room temperature. Frost if desired.

NOTE: This batter can also be baked in a 9 by 13-inch cake pan for 35 to 40 minutes.

VARIATIONS

1. PUMPKIN PECAN SPICE CAKE: Add ½ cup chopped pecans along with the flour mixture.

2. PUMPKIN DATE SPICE CAKE: Add ¾ cup chopped dates along with the flour mixture.

3. PUMPKIN RAISIN SPICE CAKE: Add ¾ cup raisins along with the flour mixture.

NUTRITIVE VALUES PER SERVING
Number of servings 16

calories 168 • carbohydrate 27 grams • protein 2 grams • fat 6 grams
sodium 196 milligrams • cholesterol 0 milligrams

Low-sodium diets: Use salt-free margarine
and low-sodium baking powder.

RAISIN SPICE CAKE

This cake can be made with golden or dark raisins, but I prefer the dark ones.

YIELD: ONE 9 BY 13-INCH CAKE

1/2 cup raisins

1 1/2 cups water

1/2 cup (1 stick) margarine

3/4 cup sugar

1/3 cup egg whites, at room temperature

3 cups all-purpose flour

1 teaspoon baking powder

1 teaspoon baking soda

2 teaspoons cinnamon

1 teaspoon allspice

Preheat oven to 350°F. Grease a 9 by 13-inch cake pan with margarine or cooking spray and set aside.

Combine raisins and water in a saucepan. Bring to a boil, reduce heat, and simmer for 2 minutes. Cool to room temperature and drain well, reserving raisins and 1 cup liquid. Add water to the liquid, if necessary, to total 1 cup liquid.

Using an electric mixer at medium speed, cream margarine and sugar together until light and fluffy. Add egg whites and mix at medium speed to blend, scraping down the bowl before and after the addition.

Stir flour, baking powder, baking soda, cinnamon, and allspice together to blend and then add to the batter, along with the reserved liquid. Mix at medium speed until creamy. Stir in the raisins.

Spread the batter evenly in the prepared pan. Bake for 50 minutes or until the cake pulls away from the sides of the pan and a cake tester inserted in the center comes out clean. Cool on a wire rack. Frost if desired.

NUTRITIVE VALUES PER SERVING

Number of servings 16

---

calories 151 • carbohydrate 25 grams • protein 3 grams • fat 5 grams
sodium 119 milligrams • cholesterol 0 milligrams

Low-sodium diets: Use salt-free margarine
and low-sodium baking powder.

SUPREME SPICE CAKE

I especially like the combination of spices in this cake. In fact, I've also used the same combination in muffins and apple pie with excellent results. You can bake the cake in a tube pan, but I think it is prettier in a Bundt pan.

*YIELD: ONE BUNDT CAKE OR
10-INCH TUBE CAKE*

½ cup (1 stick) margarine

¾ cup brown sugar

⅓ cup egg whites or liquid egg
  substitute

2¾ cups all-purpose flour

⅓ cup dry buttermilk

2 teaspoons baking powder

½ teaspoon baking soda

1 teaspoon cinnamon

1 teaspoon nutmeg

½ teaspoon ground cloves

1 cup water, at room
  temperature

¼ cup raisins

¼ cup chopped black or
  English walnuts

Preheat oven to 350°F. Grease a Bundt (fluted tube) or 10-inch tube pan with margarine or cooking spray and set aside.

Using an electric mixer at medium speed, cream margarine and brown sugar together until light and fluffy. Add egg whites or liquid egg substitute and mix at medium speed until creamy, scraping down the bowl before and after the addition.

Stir flour, dry buttermilk, baking powder, baking soda, and spices together to blend well and add, along with the water, to the creamy mixture. Mix at medium speed until creamy. Stir in raisins and nuts.

Spread the batter evenly in the prepared pan. Bake for 50 minutes or until the cake starts to pull away from the sides of the pan and a cake tester inserted in the center comes out clean. Cool in the pan on a wire rack for 10 minutes. Then turn out onto the rack to cool to room temperature. The cake may be frosted but is generally served plain or with Powdered Sugar Glaze (page 193).

NUTRITIVE VALUES PER SERVING

Number of servings 20

---

calories 159 • carbohydrate 24 grams • protein 3 grams • fat 6 grams
sodium 128 milligrams • cholesterol 1 milligram

Low-sodium diets: Use salt-free margarine
and low-sodium baking powder.

TOMATO SPICE CAKE

No one will guess that this cake, popular fifty years ago, has tomato soup in it. It is a good, spicy cake that is great served warm with Lemon or Orange Sauce (page 201) or at room temperature with Vanilla Powdered Sugar Frosting (page 192).

YIELD: ONE 9-INCH SQUARE CAKE

6 tablespoons (³/₄ stick) margarine

³/₄ cup sugar

2 large egg whites

1¹/₂ cups all-purpose flour

2 tablespoons dry buttermilk

1 teaspoon baking soda

¹/₂ teaspoon cinnamon

¹/₂ teaspoon ground cloves

¹/₂ teaspoon nutmeg

1 10³/₄-ounce can condensed tomato soup

Preheat oven to 375°F. Grease a 9-inch square cake pan with margarine or cooking spray and set aside.

Using an electric mixer at medium speed, cream margarine and sugar together until light and fluffy. Add egg whites and mix at medium speed to blend well, scraping down the bowl before and after the addition.

Stir flour, dry buttermilk, baking soda, and spices together to blend well and add to the creamy mixture, along with the soup. Beat at medium speed until smooth.

Spread evenly in the prepared pan. Bake for 30 minutes or until the cake pulls away from the sides of the pan and a cake tester inserted in the center comes out clean. Cool on a wire rack. Frost if desired.

NUTRITIVE VALUES PER SERVING

Number of servings 16

calories 134 • carbohydrate 21 grams • protein 2 grams • fat 5 grams
sodium 213 milligrams • cholesterol 0 milligrams

Low-sodium diets: Use salt-free margarine
and low-sodium soup.

FIRM

CAKES

DATE BUNDT CAKE

DOUBLE ALMOND DELIGHT CAKE

GRAHAM CRACKER CAKE

BASIC POUND CAKE

SPICE POUND CAKE

ALMOND POUND CAKE

SEED CAKE

CARAMEL POUND CAKE

LEMON POUND CAKE

ORANGE POUND CAKE

DATE BUNDT CAKE

YIELD: ONE BUNDT CAKE OR
10-INCH TUBE CAKE

1 cup chopped pitted dates	2 teaspoons baking powder
1 cup water	1 teaspoon baking soda
½ cup (1 stick) margarine	1 teaspoon salt
1½ teaspoons vanilla extract	1 cup brown sugar
1½ teaspoons lemon juice	½ cup egg whites or liquid egg substitute
3 cups all-purpose flour	

Preheat oven to 350°F. Grease a Bundt (fluted tube) or 10-inch tube pan (preferably non-stick) with margarine or cooking spray and set aside.

Combine dates, water, and margarine in a small saucepan and cook over medium heat, stirring frequently, for 5 to 8 minutes or until slightly thickened. Remove from heat, add vanilla and lemon juice, and cool to room temperature.

Place flour, baking powder, baking soda, salt, and brown sugar in the bowl of an electric mixer and mix at low speed to blend well. Add date mixture and egg whites or liquid egg substitute and mix at medium speed until creamy.

Spread the batter evenly in the prepared pan. Bake for 50 to 55 minutes or until the cake pulls away from the sides of the pan and a cake tester inserted in the center comes out clean. Cool in the pan for 10 minutes. Then turn out onto a wire rack to cool to room temperature. This cake is not generally frosted.

NUTRITIVE VALUES PER SERVING

Number of servings 20

---

calories *177* • carbohydrate *32* grams • protein *3* grams • fat *5* grams
sodium *249* milligrams • cholesterol *0* milligrams

Low-sodium diets: Omit salt.
Use salt-free margarine and low-sodium baking powder.

DOUBLE ALMOND
DELIGHT CAKE

You won't need to frost this cake. It is best served slightly warm and is excellent with coffee or tea. It freezes well and by defrosting it in the microwave, your friends will be convinced you baked it that morning.

YIELD: ONE 9 BY 13-INCH CAKE

TOPPING

½ cup slivered almonds

¼ cup sugar

2 tablespoons margarine

2 tablespoons all-purpose flour

CAKE

½ cup (1 stick) margarine

½ cup sugar

½ cup egg whites or liquid egg substitute

½ teaspoon almond extract

1 12½-ounce can Solo Almond Filling

2 cups all-purpose flour

1 teaspoon baking powder

1 teaspoon baking soda

1 cup water, at room temperature

Preheat oven to 350°F. Grease a 9 by 13-inch cake pan with margarine or cooking spray and set aside.

Prepare topping: Combine slivered almonds, sugar, margarine, and flour in the bowl of an electric mixer and mix at medium speed until crumbly. Set aside.

Using an electric mixer at medium speed, cream margarine and sugar together until light and fluffy. Add egg whites or liquid egg substitute, almond extract, and filling and mix at medium speed for 1 minute, scraping down the bowl before and after the addition.

Stir flour, baking powder, and baking soda together to blend well and add to the creamed mixture, along with the water. Mix at medium speed for 1 minute.

Spread the batter evenly in the prepared pan. Sprinkle the reserved crumb mixture evenly over the batter, leaving a ¼-inch border without crumb mixture.

Bake for 35 minutes or until the cake pulls away from the sides of the pan and a cake tester inserted in the center comes out clean. Serve warm.

NUTRITIVE VALUES PER SERVING

Number of servings 24

---

calories 170 • carbohydrate 24 grams • protein 2 grams • fat 8 grams
sodium 130 milligrams • cholesterol 0 milligrams

Low-sodium diets: Use salt-free margarine
and low-sodium baking powder.

GRAHAM CRACKER CAKE

Graham cracker crumbs replace flour in this recipe, giving it an unusual texture. It is rather heavy and coarse, but the flavor is excellent. It appeals to those who enjoy graham crackers.

YIELD: ONE BUNDT CAKE OR 10-INCH TUBE CAKE

½ cup (1 stick) margarine

1 cup sugar

1 cup egg whites or liquid egg substitute

1 teaspoon vanilla extract

1 pound graham cracker crumbs

1 teaspoon baking powder

1 teaspoon baking soda

2 tablespoons instant nonfat dry milk

1 cup water, at room temperature

Preheat oven to 350°F. Grease and flour a Bundt (fluted tube) or 10-inch tube pan (preferably non-stick) and set aside.

Using an electric mixer at medium speed, cream margarine and sugar together until light and fluffy. Add egg whites or liquid egg substitute and vanilla and mix at medium speed until creamy, scraping down the bowl before and after the addition.

Stir crumbs, baking powder, baking soda, and dry milk together to blend well and add, along with the water, to the creamy mixture. Mix at medium speed until smooth.

Spread the batter evenly in the prepared pan. Bake for 1 hour or until a cake tester inserted in the center comes out clean. Cool in the pan on a wire rack for 10 minutes. Then turn out onto the rack and let cool to room temperature. This cake is not generally frosted.

NOTE: If packaged graham cracker crumbs are not available, use a food processor or a heavy rolling pin to crush 1 pound graham crackers to fine crumbs.

NUTRITIVE VALUES PER SERVING

Number of servings 20

---

calories 134 • carbohydrate 19 grams • protein 2 grams • fat 5 grams
sodium 202 milligrams • cholesterol 0 milligrams

Low-sodium diets: Use salt-free margarine
and low-sodium baking powder.

BASIC POUND CAKE

Pound cakes date back to the seventeenth century, when the basic ingredients included a pound each of sugar, butter, and flour, along with flavorings such as rose water or candied violets. These cakes were a luxury available only to the very wealthy, served only on noteworthy occasions, and regarded as very special.

YIELD: ONE 9 BY 5 BY 3-INCH LOAF CAKE

½ cup (1 stick) margarine

1 cup sugar

1 cup liquid egg substitute,
  at room temperature

½ teaspoon vanilla extract

½ teaspoon almond extract

2 cups all-purpose flour

1 teaspoon baking powder

¼ teaspoon salt

Preheat oven to 325°F. Grease a 9 by 5 by 3-inch loaf pan with margarine or cooking spray and set aside.

Using an electric mixer at medium speed, cream margarine and sugar together until light and fluffy. Add liquid egg substitute and flavorings and mix at medium speed for 30 seconds, scraping down the bowl before and after the addition.

Stir flour, baking powder, and salt together to blend well and add to the egg substitute mixture. Mix at medium speed until creamy. Spread the batter evenly in the prepared pan. Bake for 1 hour and 15 minutes or until the cake pulls away from the sides of the pan and a cake tester inserted in the center comes out clean. Cool in the pan on a wire rack for 15 minutes. Then turn out onto the rack to cool to room temperature.

NOTE: This cake can use egg whites instead of liquid egg substitute, but it won't have the characteristic yellow color of pound cake.

VARIATIONS

1. SPICE POUND CAKE: Add ½ teaspoon cinnamon, ½ teaspoon nutmeg, and ¼ teaspoon ground cloves to the flour mixture.

2. ALMOND POUND CAKE: Add ½ cup finely chopped almonds to the flour mixture.

3. SEED CAKE: Omit almond flavoring and add 1 tablespoon caraway or anise seed along with the flour.

NUTRITIVE VALUES PER SERVING

Number of servings 18

---

calories 138 • carbohydrate 22 grams • protein 1 gram • fat 5 grams
sodium 107 milligrams • cholesterol 0 milligrams

Low-sodium diets: Omit salt.
Use salt-free margarine and low-sodium baking powder.

CARAMEL POUND CAKE

YIELD: ONE 9 BY 5 BY 3-INCH LOAF CAKE

½ cup (1 stick) margarine

1 cup brown sugar

1 cup egg whites or liquid egg
substitute, at room
temperature

1 teaspoon caramel or burnt
sugar flavoring

2 cups all-purpose flour

¼ cup dry buttermilk

½ teaspoon baking powder

½ teaspoon baking soda

¼ teaspoon salt

⅓ cup water, at room
temperature

Preheat oven to 350°F. Grease a 9 by 5 by 3-inch loaf pan with margarine
or cooking spray and set aside.

Using an electric mixer at medium speed, cream margarine and brown
sugar together until light and fluffy. Add egg whites or liquid egg substi-

tute and caramel or burnt sugar flavoring and beat at medium speed for 30 seconds, scraping down the bowl before and after the addition.

Stir flour, dry buttermilk, baking powder, baking soda, and salt together to blend well and add to the egg mixture, along with the water. Beat at medium speed until creamy.

Spread the batter evenly in the prepared pan. Bake for 1 hour and 15 minutes or until the cake pulls away from the sides of the pan and a cake tester inserted in the center comes out clean. Cool in the pan on a wire rack for 15 minutes. Then turn out onto the rack to cool to room temperature.

NUTRITIVE VALUES PER SERVING
Number of servings 18

---

calories 154 • carbohydrate 23 grams • protein 3 grams • fat 5 grams
sodium 157 milligrams • cholesterol 1 milligram

Low-sodium diets: Omit salt.
Use salt-free margarine and low-sodium baking powder.

LEMON POUND CAKE

It is so much simpler to make a pound cake now than it was before we had electric mixers. I hate to think of how they used to cream the butter by hand and then add the eggs and beat them some more. The poor cooks must have been exhausted when they finally put the cake in the oven.

YIELD: ONE 9 BY 5 BY 3-INCH LOAF CAKE

½ cup (1 stick) margarine

1 cup sugar

1 cup egg whites, at room
 temperature

1 teaspoon lemon extract

1 tablespoon grated fresh or
 finely chopped dried lemon
 rind

2 cups all-purpose flour

1 teaspoon baking powder

¼ teaspoon salt

⅓ cup water, at room
 temperature

Preheat oven to 350°F. Grease a 9 by 5 by 3-inch loaf pan with margarine or cooking spray and set aside.

Using an electric mixer at medium speed, cream margarine and sugar together until light and fluffy. Add egg whites, lemon extract, and lemon rind and mix at low speed for 30 seconds, scraping down the bowl before and after the addition.

Stir flour, baking powder, and salt together and add to the egg white mixture, along with the water. Mix at medium speed until creamy.

Spread the batter evenly in the prepared pan. Bake for 1 hour and 15 minutes or until the cake pulls away from the sides of the pan and a cake tester inserted in the center comes out clean. Cool in the pan on a wire rack for 15 minutes. Then turn out onto the rack and cool to room temperature.

VARIATION

ORANGE POUND CAKE: Substitute 1 teaspoon orange extract and 1 tablespoon orange rind for the lemon extract and rind.

NUTRITIVE VALUES PER SERVING

Number of servings 18

---

calories 145 • carbohydrate 22 grams • protein 3 grams • fat 5 grams
sodium 129 milligrams • cholesterol 0 milligrams

Low-sodium diets: Omit salt.
Use salt-free margarine and low-sodium baking powder.

CUPCAKES

BANANA CUPCAKES

BANANA NUT CUPCAKES

BANANA RAISIN CUPCAKES

BLUEBERRY CUPCAKES

BROWNIE CUPCAKES

DARK CHOCOLATE CUPCAKES

LIGHT CHOCOLATE CUPCAKES

HONEY TEA CAKES

LEMON CUPCAKES

ORANGE CUPCAKES

OAT BRAN CUPCAKES

SPICE CUPCAKES

WHITE CUPCAKES

RAISIN CUPCAKES

LICORICE CUPCAKES

YELLOW CUPCAKES

DATE CUPCAKES

ALMOND CUPCAKES

Cupcakes are versatile and can be served in many ways. Dainty ones are nice for a tea or a ladies' luncheon and larger ones can be decorated for parties. They are handy to tuck into lunch bags and are just right for an afternoon snack.

Almost any cake batter can be used for cupcakes except angel food cake — and even that can be used in an emergency. The batter for a 9-inch square cake will make a dozen cupcakes and the batter for a 9 by 13-inch cake will give you two dozen smaller cupcakes. To convert a cupcake recipe to a cake recipe, keep in mind that the batter for a dozen cupcakes will make a 9-inch square cake and that the batter for two dozen cupcakes will make a 9 by 13-inch cake, three 8-inch layers, or two 9-inch layers (three if you want them thin). Naturally, the baking times will need adjusting. When converting from cupcakes to a single larger cake, add five to ten minutes baking time. To convert from a larger cake to cupcakes, subtract five or ten minutes from the baking time for the cake. All the cupcakes should have a uniform color and a cake tester should come out clean when inserted in the center of the cupcakes. Also, please review the seven basic rules for cake baking in Cake Preparation (page 5).

I bake cupcakes in muffin tins with silicone-treated paper liners. (I don't use untreated paper liners because I find too much of the cake sticks to the paper.) You can buy silicone-treated liners in specialty kitchen supply stores or from Maid of Scandinavia, 3244 Raleigh Avenue, Minneapolis, MN 55416. For a small fee they will send you their catalog, which includes many interesting supplies for your kitchen.

I often use a dipper for measuring cupcake batter because it helps keep the cupcakes the same size. The size of a dipper is based on the number of dippers in a quart, which has 64 tablespoons. A No. 16 dipper is $1/16$th of a quart, or 4 tablespoons ($1/4$ cup); a No. 20 dipper is $1/20$th of a quart, or 3 tablespoons; a No. 40 is $1/40$th of a quart, or $1\frac{1}{2}$ tablespoons; and a No. 60 is $1/60$th of a quart, or 1 tablespoon. You can buy dippers at a good hardware store or from

Maid of Scandinavia. Numbers 16 and 20 are the most useful for cupcakes; numbers 40 and 60 are the right size for cookies.

I haven't included any frostings in this chapter, although cupcakes are generally frosted when served. (It is always fun to decorate cupcakes for children's parties or special occasions.) Thus the nutritive information with the cupcakes is for the cupcakes only. If you use any of the recipes from Frostings and Sauces, remember to add the nutritive value to the value of the cupcake.

Please review the seven basic rules for cake baking in Cake Preparation (page 5) before making any of the cupcakes in this chapter.

BANANA CUPCAKES

YIELD: 18 CUPCAKES

½ cup (1 stick) margarine

1 cup sugar

1 teaspoon vanilla extract

¼ cup egg whites or liquid egg substitute, at room temperature

2 medium bananas

2 cups all-purpose flour

1 tablespoon dry buttermilk

1 teaspoon baking soda

¼ teaspoon salt

¼ cup water, at room temperature

Preheat oven to 350°F. Grease three 6-cup muffin tins with margarine or cooking spray, or line with paper liners. Set aside.

Using an electric mixer at medium speed, cream margarine and sugar together until light and fluffy. Add vanilla and egg whites or liquid egg substitute. Mix at medium speed until creamy, scraping down the bowl before and after the addition. Slice bananas thin and add to the creamy mixture. Mix at medium speed until nearly smooth.

Stir flour, dry buttermilk, baking soda, and salt together to blend well and add to the banana mixture, along with the water. Mix at medium speed until creamy.

Fill the prepared muffin tins with batter about halfway (or use a level No. 20 dipper). Bake for 25 to 30 minutes or until lightly browned and a cake tester inserted in the center of a cupcake comes out clean. Cool on a wire rack.

VARIATIONS

1. BANANA NUT CUPCAKES: Add ¾ cup chopped nuts along with the flour.

2. BANANA RAISIN CUPCAKES: Add ¾ cup raisins along with the flour.

NUTRITIVE VALUES PER SERVING
Number of servings 18

---

calories 153 • carbohydrate 25 grams • protein 2 grams • fat 5 grams
sodium 172 milligrams • cholesterol 0 milligrams

Low-sodium diets: Omit salt
and use salt-free margarine.

BLUEBERRY CUPCAKES

This isn't really blueberry country, but I like blueberries and use them frequently, since I can get such wonderful frozen ones at my local grocery store.

YIELD: 12 CUPCAKES

1½ cups all-purpose flour

½ cup sugar

2 tablespoons dry buttermilk

1½ teaspoons finely grated fresh or finely chopped dried orange rind

1½ teaspoons baking powder

½ teaspoon baking soda

¼ teaspoon salt

1 cup water, at room temperature

⅓ cup vegetable oil

1 large egg white or 2 tablespoons liquid egg substitute

1¼ cups unsweetened fresh or frozen blueberries

Preheat oven to 375°F. Grease a 12-cup muffin tin with margarine or cooking spray, or line with paper liners. Set aside.

Place flour, sugar, dry buttermilk, orange rind, baking powder, baking soda, and salt in the bowl of an electric mixer and mix at low speed to blend well. Beat water, oil, and egg white or liquid egg substitute together to blend and add to flour mixture. Mix until creamy. Stir in the blueberries.

Fill the prepared muffin tins with batter about halfway (or use a level No. 20 dipper). Bake for 25 to 30 minutes or until browned and firm. Cool on a wire rack.

NUTRITIVE VALUES PER SERVING

Number of servings 12

---

calories 157 • carbohydrate 23 grams • protein 2 grams • fat 6 grams
sodium 132 milligrams • cholesterol 1 milligram

Low-sodium diets: Omit salt
and use low-sodium baking powder.

BROWNIE CUPCAKES

I call these brownie cupcakes because they have the deep, rich chocolate taste of brownies. The addition of nuts and raisins makes them even more special.

YIELD: 12 CUPCAKES

$^3/_4$ **cup all-purpose flour**

1 cup sugar

$^1/_2$ **cup cocoa**

2 tablespoons instant nonfat dry milk

1 teaspoon baking powder

$^1/_2$ **teaspoon salt**

$^1/_2$ **cup egg whites or liquid egg substitute**

$^1/_3$ **cup vegetable oil**

1 teaspoon vanilla extract

$^1/_2$ **cup water, at room temperature**

$^1/_4$ **cup chopped English walnuts**

$^1/_4$ **cup raisins**

Preheat oven to 350°F. Grease a 12-cup muffin tin with margarine or cooking spray, or line with paper liners. Set aside.

Place flour, sugar, cocoa, dry milk, baking powder, and salt in the bowl of an electric mixer and mix at low speed to blend. Beat egg whites or liquid egg substitute, oil, vanilla, and water together with a fork to blend and add, along with the nuts and raisins, to the flour mixture. Mix at medium speed until shiny.

Spoon about 2½ tablespoons (a scant No. 20 dipper) of batter into each of the prepared muffin cups. Bake for 20 minutes or until a cake tester inserted in the center of a cupcake comes out clean. (Do not overbake.) Cool on a wire rack.

NUTRITIVE VALUES PER SERVING

Number of servings 12

calories 185 • carbohydrate 28 grams • protein 3 grams • fat 8 grams
sodium 138 milligrams • cholesterol 0 milligrams

Low-sodium diets: Omit salt
and use low-sodium baking powder.

DARK CHOCOLATE CUPCAKES

These cupcakes aren't very large, but I like the texture and love the flavor.

YIELD: 12 CUPCAKES

$1/2$ cup sugar

$1/3$ cup cocoa

$1/3$ cup vegetable oil

$1/4$ cup egg whites or liquid egg substitute

1 tablespoon vinegar

$1^1/2$ cups all-purpose flour

1 teaspoon baking powder

1 teaspoon baking soda

$1/4$ teaspoon salt

$1^1/4$ cups warm water

Preheat oven to 350°F. Grease a 12-cup muffin tin with margarine or cooking spray, or line with paper liners. Set aside.

Place sugar, cocoa, oil, egg whites or liquid egg substitute, and vinegar in the bowl of an electric mixer and mix at medium speed until thick and glossy.

Stir flour, baking powder, baking soda, and salt together to blend well and add to the glossy mixture, along with the water. Mix at medium speed for $1^1/2$ minutes or until smooth and lighter colored.

Fill the prepared muffin tins with batter about halfway (or use a level No. 20 dipper). Bake for 25 to 30 minutes or until a cake tester inserted in the center of a cupcake comes out clean. Cool on a wire rack.

NUTRITIVE VALUES PER SERVING

Number of servings 12

---

calories 151 • carbohydrate 22 grams • protein 3 grams • fat 7 grams
sodium 149 milligrams • cholesterol 0 milligrams

Low-sodium diets: Omit salt
and use low-sodium baking powder.

LIGHT CHOCOLATE CUPCAKES

*I thought about calling these milk chocolate cupcakes because they are light in color,
but I decided to call them light chocolate cupcakes because of the buttermilk in them.*

YIELD: 12 CUPCAKES

2 cups all-purpose flour

1 cup sugar

¹/₄ cup cocoa

2 tablespoons dry buttermilk

1 teaspoon baking soda

¹/₄ teaspoon salt

**¹/₄ cup egg whites or liquid egg
substitute**

¹/₃ cup vegetable oil

1 teaspoon vanilla extract

¹/₂ cup hot water

Preheat oven to 350°F. Grease a 12-cup muffin tin with margarine or
cooking spray, or line with paper liners. Set aside.

Place flour, sugar, cocoa, dry buttermilk, baking soda, and salt in the
bowl of an electric mixer and mix at low speed for 30 seconds to blend.

Stir egg whites or liquid egg substitute, oil, and vanilla together and add to the flour mixture, along with the water. Mix at medium speed just to blend.

Fill the prepared muffin tins with batter about two-thirds full (or use a level No. 16 dipper). Bake for 25 to 30 minutes or until a cake tester inserted in the center of a cupcake comes out clean. Cool on a wire rack.

NUTRITIVE VALUES PER SERVING

Number of servings 12

---

calories 205 • carbohydrate 34 grams • protein 3 grams • fat 7 grams
sodium 129 milligrams • cholesterol 1 milligram

Low-sodium diets: Omit salt.

HONEY TEA CAKES

These delicious spiced cupcakes are just right for an afternoon tea or coffee break. They can be frosted or served with jam or orange marmalade.

YIELD: 12 CUPCAKES

¹/₂ cup honey

¹/₂ cup brown sugar

¹/₂ cup (1 stick) margarine

¹/₄ cup egg whites or liquid egg substitute

2 cups all-purpose flour

1 teaspoon cream of tartar

¹/₂ teaspoon baking soda

1 teaspoon cardamom

1 teaspoon cinnamon

¹/₃ cup water, at room temperature

Preheat oven to 350°F. Grease a 12-cup muffin tin with margarine or cooking spray, or line with paper liners. Set aside.

Place honey, brown sugar, and margarine in the bowl of an electric mixer and mix at medium speed until creamy. Add egg whites or liquid egg substitute and mix at medium speed for 30 seconds, scraping down the bowl before and after the addition.

Stir flour, cream of tartar, baking soda, cardamom, and cinnamon together to blend well and add to the honey mixture, along with the water.

Fill the prepared muffin tins with batter about two-thirds full (or use a generous No. 16 dipper). Bake for 25 to 30 minutes or until lightly browned and a cake tester inserted in the center of a cupcake comes out clean. Cool on a wire rack.

NUTRITIVE VALUES PER SERVING
Number of servings 12

---

calories 223 • carbohydrate 36 grams • protein 4 grams • fat 8 grams
sodium 127 milligrams • cholesterol 0 milligrams

Low-sodium diets: Use salt-free margarine.

LEMON CUPCAKES

YIELD: 12 CUPCAKES

½ cup (1 stick) margarine

⅔ cup sugar

1½ teaspoons lemon extract

Grated rind of 1 large lemon or 1 tablespoon finely chopped dried lemon rind

⅓ cup egg whites or liquid egg substitute

2 cups cake flour

1 tablespoon dry buttermilk

1 teaspoon baking powder

½ teaspoon baking soda

¾ cup water, at room temperature

Preheat oven to 350°F. Grease a 12-cup muffin tin with margarine or cooking spray, or line with paper liners. Set aside.

Using an electric mixer at medium speed, cream margarine and sugar together until light and fluffy. Add lemon extract, lemon rind, and egg whites or liquid egg substitute and mix at medium speed for 30 seconds, scraping down the bowl before and after the addition.

Stir flour, dry buttermilk, baking powder, and baking soda together to blend well and add to the egg mixture, along with the water. Mix at medium speed until creamy.

Fill the prepared muffin tins with batter about halfway (or use a level No. 20 dipper). Bake for 25 to 30 minutes or until lightly browned. Cool on a wire rack.

VARIATION

ORANGE CUPCAKES: Substitute orange extract and rind for lemon extract and rind.

NUTRITIVE VALUES PER SERVING

Number of servings 12

---

calories 191 • carbohydrate 27 grams • protein 3 grams • fat 8 grams
sodium 210 milligrams • cholesterol 0 milligrams

Low-sodium diets: Use salt-free margarine
and low-sodium baking powder.

OAT BRAN CUPCAKES

These luscious cupcakes have almost as much fiber as oat bran muffins.

YIELD: 12 CUPCAKES

1 cup oat bran cereal

1 cup water

1/3 cup vegetable oil

2 large egg whites or 1/4 cup
  liquid egg substitute

1 teaspoon maple flavoring

1 tablespoon lemon juice

1 1/4 cups all-purpose flour

1/2 cup brown sugar

1 teaspoon baking soda

1/4 teaspoon salt

1/2 cup raisins

Preheat oven to 375°F. Grease a 12-cup muffin tin with margarine or cooking spray, or line with paper liners. Set aside.

Place cereal, water, oil, egg whites or liquid egg substitute, maple flavoring, and lemon juice in the bowl of an electric mixer, mix well, and let stand for 45 minutes.

Stir flour, brown sugar, baking soda, salt, and raisins together to blend well and add to the bran mixture. Mix at medium speed until creamy.

Fill the prepared muffin tins with batter a little over halfway (or use a scant No. 16 dipper). Bake for 25 to 30 minutes or until firm and a cake tester inserted in the center of a cupcake comes out clean. Cool on a wire rack.

NUTRITIVE VALUES PER SERVING

Number of servings 12

---

calories 182 • carbohydrate 28 grams • protein 3 grams • fat 7 grams
sodium 127 milligrams • cholesterol 0 milligrams

Low-sodium diets: Omit salt.

SPICE CUPCAKES

YIELD: 12 CUPCAKES

6 tablespoons (³/4 stick) margarine

³/4 cup brown sugar

2 large egg whites or ¹/4 cup liquid egg substitute

2 cups cake flour

2 teaspoons baking powder

¹/4 teaspoon salt

1 teaspoon cinnamon

¹/4 teaspoon ginger

¹/4 teaspoon ground cloves

1 cup water, at room temperature

Preheat oven to 375°F. Grease a 12-cup muffin tin with margarine or cooking spray, or line with paper liners. Set aside.

Using an electric mixer at medium speed, cream margarine and brown sugar together until light and fluffy. Add egg whites or liquid egg substitute and beat at medium speed until creamy, scraping down the bowl before and after the addition.

Stir the flour, baking powder, salt, and spices together to blend well and add, along with the water, to the egg mixture. Beat at medium speed until creamy.

Fill the prepared muffin tins with batter about halfway (or use a generous No. 20 dipper). Bake for 20 to 25 minutes or until a cake tester inserted in the center of a cupcake comes out clean. Cool on a wire rack.

NUTRITIVE VALUES PER SERVING

Number of servings 12

---

calories 163 • carbohydrate 26 grams • protein 2 grams • fat 6 grams
sodium 180 milligrams • cholesterol 0 milligrams

Low-sodium diets: Omit salt.
Use salt-free margarine and low-sodium baking powder.

WHITE CUPCAKES

This basic cupcake recipe lends itself easily to the addition of raisins and nuts and can be beautifully decorated for special occasions.

YIELD: 12 CUPCAKES

½ cup (1 stick) margarine

1 cup sugar

¼ cup egg whites

1½ teaspoons vanilla extract

1¾ cups cake flour

1 tablespoon instant nonfat dry
  milk

1½ teaspoons baking powder

¼ teaspoon salt

¾ cup water, at room
  temperature

Preheat oven to 375°F. Grease a 12-cup muffin tin with margarine or cooking spray, or line with paper liners. Set aside.

Using an electric mixer at medium speed, cream margarine and sugar together until light and fluffy. Add egg whites and vanilla to the creamed mixture and mix at medium speed until light and fluffy, scraping down the bowl before and after the addition.

Stir flour, dry milk, baking powder, and salt together to blend well and add to the creamy mixture, along with the water. Mix at medium speed until creamy.

Fill the prepared muffin tins with batter about halfway (or use a level No. 20 dipper). Bake for 25 to 30 minutes or until lightly browned and a cake tester inserted in the center of a cupcake comes out clean. Cool on a wire rack. Frost if desired.

VARIATIONS

1. RAISIN CUPCAKES: Add ¹/₂ cup raisins along with the flour.

2. LICORICE CUPCAKES: Add 2 drops red food coloring and 1 teaspoon anise flavoring or 1 tablespoon anise seed.

NUTRITIVE VALUES PER SERVING

Number of servings 12

---

calories 187 • carbohydrate 28 grams • protein 2 grams • fat 7 grams
sodium 185 milligrams • cholesterol 0 milligrams

Low-sodium diets: Omit salt.
Use salt-free margarine and low-sodium baking powder.

YELLOW CUPCAKES

I used liquid egg substitute to give these cupcakes their yellow color. If you prefer, you can use an equal amount of egg whites and a couple of drops of yellow food coloring.

YIELD: 12 CUPCAKES

1³/₄ cups cake flour

1 cup sugar

1 tablespoon instant nonfat dry milk

1¹/₂ teaspoons baking powder

¹/₂ cup (1 stick) margarine, softened

¹/₃ cup liquid egg substitute

1¹/₂ teaspoons vanilla extract

³/₄ cup water, at room temperature

Preheat oven to 375°F. Grease a 12-cup muffin tin with margarine or cooking spray, or line with paper liners.

Place flour, sugar, dry milk, and baking powder in the bowl of an electric mixer and mix at low speed for 30 seconds to blend well. Add margarine, liquid egg substitute, vanilla, and water to dry mixture and mix at medium speed until smooth.

Fill the prepared muffin tins with batter about halfway (or use a level No. 20 dipper). Bake for 25 to 30 minutes or until lightly browned and a cake tester inserted in the center of a cupcake comes out clean. Cool on a wire rack.

VARIATIONS

1. DATE CUPCAKES: Add ½ cup finely chopped dates along with the flour.

2. ALMOND CUPCAKES: Omit vanilla and add 1 teaspoon almond extract. Add ½ cup slivered almonds to the batter just before it is put into the muffin tins.

NUTRITIVE VALUES PER SERVING

Number of servings 12

---

calories 187 • carbohydrate 28 grams • protein 3 grams • fat 7 grams
sodium 162 milligrams • cholesterol 0 milligrams

Low-sodium diets: Use salt-free margarine
and low-sodium baking powder.

CAKES FOR
SPECIAL OCCASIONS

CHOCOLATE MERINGUE CAKE

STRAWBERRY CHOCOLATE MERINGUE CAKE

LADY BALTIMORE CAKE

LORD BALTIMORE CAKE

POPPYSEED TORTE

PRINCE OF WALES CAKE

SACHER TORTE

PEACH UPSIDE-DOWN CAKE

PINEAPPLE UPSIDE-DOWN CAKE

APRICOT NUT UPSIDE-DOWN CAKE

BANANA WALNUT FRUITCAKE

BOURBON FRUITCAKE

CHOCOLATE FRUITCAKE

IRISH FRUITCAKE

ORANGE FRUITCAKE

GRAND MARNIER FRUITCAKE

REGENIA'S FRUITCAKE

Many countries have cakes that are reserved for special occasions such as birthdays, anniversaries, holidays, and other memorable events. Some of them could be included in European-style Cakes, but I have included them here because, although I have cut both the fat and sugar, these cakes are higher in fat and sugar than any I would ordinarily prepare. You can use them for holidays or parties and to impress your family and friends. In fact, these cakes are so good, you might even start a new family tradition. I truly love to make them, though I limit myself to a small portion of any of them.

Also included in this chapter are fruitcakes, which are special cakes generally reserved for holidays or for the groom's cake at weddings. I have lowered the fat and sugar content in these cakes, but they still have quite a bit of sugar in them because of the candied fruit. In general, candied fruit has almost as much sugar, ounce for ounce, as pure sugar. I usually serve thin slices of fruitcake as a special treat, but I certainly don't serve it for everyday eating, even if it is cholesterol-free. Some people joke about the unpopularity of fruitcake, but I find that if a fruitcake is well made, most people will enjoy it.

Another myth about fruitcakes is that they are hard to make. Fruitcakes are easy to prepare once you learn that they need steam in the oven to help keep the crust soft. At professional bakeries, bakers use a steam valve to regulate the amount of steam in the ovens. In home kitchens, however, we need to find other ways to provide steam. Some people put a shallow pan on the bottom shelf of the oven and pour boiling water into it to form steam while the cake is baking. I find that more than a little cumbersome and dangerous, so I put a 9 by 13-inch cake pan filled with warm water on the bottom shelf of the oven. I turn the oven up to 400°F and wait for the water to boil. When it does, I turn the oven to the correct temperature for the fruitcake and put the cake in the oven. The water continues to provide enough steam for the cake and I get the softer crust I want. I let the pan of water cool in the oven before I remove it.

Most fruitcakes are moistened with fruit juice or some kind of liquor. Some cooks direct you to wrap fruitcakes in linen that has been moistened with fruit juice or liquor, but I find that a cake that has been moistened, wrapped in aluminum foil, allowed to mellow for a time, and then frozen will keep as well as, or better than, a cake wrapped in a piece of juice- or liquor-soaked linen.

One last note: Fruitcakes tend to stick to the pans they are baked in, so I recommend using pans with a non-stick surface. If the pan is sprayed with cooking spray or greased with margarine and the cake is allowed to rest in the pan for 10 or 15 minutes after baking, the cake will come out of the pan easily. Pans without a non-stick surface have to be greased, lined with brown or waxed paper, and greased again. I have included in the directions the conventional method for preparing pans without a non-stick surface. If, however, you use a non-stick pan, simply grease the pan once and disregard the instructions to line with waxed paper and grease again.

Please review the seven basic rules for cake baking in Cake Preparation (page 5) before making any of the cakes in this chapter.

CHOCOLATE MERINGUE CAKE

This cake is not difficult to make, but it does require coordinating the various steps. To simplify the preparation, measure the ingredients before starting to cook.

YIELD: THREE 9-INCH LAYERS

MERINGUE

1/2 cup egg whites, at room
  temperature
1/2 teaspoon cream of tartar
1/4 teaspoon salt
1 teaspoon almond extract
1 cup sugar
1/2 cup sliced or chopped
  almonds

CAKE

1/2 cup egg whites or liquid egg
  substitute, at room
  temperature

1/3 cup vegetable oil
1 cup sugar
2 teaspoons vanilla extract
2 1/4 cups all-purpose flour
1/4 cup cocoa
2 tablespoons instant nonfat
  dry milk
2 teaspoons baking soda
1/2 teaspoon salt
2 cups hot water
.92-ounce Featherweight
  whipped topping
17 whole almonds

Preheat oven to 350°F. Grease three 9-inch layer cake pans with margarine or cooking spray and line with waxed paper circles. Set aside.

Prepare the meringue: Using an electric mixer with a whip attachment, whip egg whites, cream of tartar, salt, and almond extract together at high speed until the mixture holds soft peaks. Gradually add the sugar, while continuing to beat at high speed, until firm and glossy. Then, using a large spoon or rubber spatula, fold the almonds into the meringue. Set aside.

Place egg whites or liquid egg substitute, oil, sugar, and vanilla in the bowl of an electric mixer and mix at low speed to blend well.

Stir flour, cocoa, dry milk, baking soda, and salt together to blend well and add, along with the water, to the egg and oil mixture. Mix at medium speed for 1 minute.

Pour one-third of the batter into each of the prepared cake pans. Top the batter in two of the three pans with half each of the reserved meringue mixture. Bake all three layers for 30 minutes or until a cake tester inserted in the center of each layer comes out clean.

Cool in the pans on a wire rack. After 10 minutes, remove the layer without the meringue from the pan and remove the waxed paper immediately. Cool the other two layers in the pans to room temperature. Run a knife around the edges of the layers and turn them out onto the rack. Remove the waxed paper and turn the layers meringue side up.

Prepare the whipped topping as directed on the packet. Then assemble the cake: Spread one of the meringue-topped layers with 1/2 cup whipped topping. Place the second meringue-topped layer on top of the first. Spread with another 1/2 cup whipped topping. Place the plain layer on top and use the rest of the whipped topping to frost the cake. Garnish with the whole almonds. Place one almond in the center of the cake and arrange the other almonds around the edge of the cake so each portion will have an almond on it.

NOTE: The cake layers may be prepared in advance but should not be frosted until just before serving.

VARIATION

STRAWBERRY CHOCOLATE MERINGUE CAKE: Spread 1/2 cup strawberry jam on top of each of the meringue-topped layers before filling and frosting with the whipped topping. Garnish with fresh strawberries instead of almonds.

NUTRITIVE VALUES PER SERVING

Number of servings 16

---

calories 253 • carbohydrate 41 grams • protein 5 grams • fat 8 grams
sodium 242 milligrams • cholesterol 0 milligrams

Low-sodium diets: Omit salt.

LADY BALTIMORE CAKE

This cake became popular in the early 1900s when Owen Wister featured it in Lady
Baltimore, *his novel about Southern society. He discussed the cake at great length
in the book and it soon became a favorite recipe across the country. When I was a
little girl my mother made it for the wedding of a favorite cousin. It was so well
received that she always made it again whenever the couple visited for their
anniversary.*

YIELD: TWO 9-INCH LAYERS

White Cake (page 83)   **¹/₄ cup chopped pecans**
White Mountain Frosting (page   **¹/₄ cup chopped dried figs**
  188)
¹/₄ cup raisins

Prepare two cake layers according to the recipe. Remove from the pans
and cool to room temperature before frosting.

Prepare White Mountain Frosting according to the recipe; add raisins,
pecans, and figs to one-third of the frosting and spread it evenly on top of

one of the layers. Top with the second layer and frost the cake with the remaining frosting.

VARIATION

LORD BALTIMORE CAKE: Omit raisins and dried figs and add ¼ cup well-drained, chopped maraschino cherries to the frosting along with the pecans.

NUTRITIVE VALUES PER SERVING

Number of servings 16

---

calories 265 • carbohydrate 48 grams • protein 4 grams • fat 7 grams
sodium 185 milligrams • cholesterol 0 milligrams

Low-sodium diets: Use the low-sodium version
of both cake and frosting.

POPPYSEED TORTE

I can't decide whether I like this torte or Poppyseed Cake (page 67) better. They have about the same ingredients but such different textures.

YIELD: THREE 9-INCH LAYERS

½ cup (1 stick) margarine

½ cup sugar

¾ cup egg whites or liquid egg substitute

1 teaspoon lemon extract

1 12½-ounce can Solo Poppy Filling

3 cups all-purpose flour

2 teaspoons baking powder

1 teaspoon baking soda

1 12-ounce can evaporated skim milk

1 cup apricot jam

1 cup Vanilla Powdered Sugar Frosting (page 192)

Preheat oven to 350°F. Grease three 9-inch layer cake pans with margarine or cooking spray and line with waxed paper circles. Set aside.

Using an electric mixer at medium speed, cream margarine and sugar together until light and fluffy. Add egg whites or liquid egg substitute, lemon extract, and poppy filling and mix at medium speed until blended, scraping down the bowl before and after the addition.

Stir flour, baking powder, and baking soda together to blend and add, along with the milk, to the creamy mixture. Mix at medium speed for 1 minute.

Spread one-third of the batter in each of the prepared pans. Bake for 30 to 35 minutes or until the layers pull away from the sides of the pans and a cake tester inserted in the center of each layer comes out clean. Cool the layers in the pans for 5 minutes. Then turn out onto a wire rack, remove the waxed paper, and cool to room temperature.

When the layers are cool, spread $1/2$ cup jam on top of one of the layers. Top with another layer, the remaining $1/2$ cup jam, then the third layer. Frost with the Vanilla Powdered Sugar Frosting.

NUTRITIVE VALUES PER SERVING

Number of servings 16

---

calories 354 • carbohydrate 60 grams • protein 9 grams • fat 9 grams
sodium 254 milligrams • cholesterol 1 milligram

Low-sodium diets: Omit salt from frosting.
Use salt-free margarine and low-sodium baking powder.

PRINCE OF WALES CAKE

The traditional recipe for this cake is much spicier than I like. To re-create the original very spicy cake, double the amount of cloves and add ¹/₂ teaspoon allspice.

YIELD: TWO 9-INCH LAYERS

CAKE

¹/₂ cup (1 stick) margarine

¹/₂ cup sugar

¹/₄ cup molasses

3 large egg whites, at room temperature

2 cups cake flour

1 teaspoon cinnamon

¹/₂ teaspoon ground cloves

1 teaspoon baking powder

1 teaspoon baking soda

1 cup strong coffee, at room temperature

1 cup Lemon Buttercream Frosting (page 190)

FILLING

¹/₂ cup sugar

3 tablespoons cornstarch

¹/₈ teaspoon salt

¹/₄ cup liquid egg substitute (not egg whites)

³/₄ cup water

1 tablespoon margarine

3 tablespoons lemon juice

Preheat oven to 350°F. Grease two 9-inch cake pans with margarine or cooking spray.

Prepare the cake: Using an electric mixer at medium speed, cream margarine, sugar, and molasses together until light and fluffy. Add egg whites and beat 1 minute at medium speed, scraping down the bowl before and after the addition.

Stir flour, cinnamon, cloves, baking powder, and baking soda together to blend well and add to the egg mixture, along with the coffee. Beat at medium speed until creamy.

Spread half of the batter in each of the prepared pans. Bake for 30 minutes or until the layers pull away from the sides of the pans and a cake tester inserted in the center of each layer comes out clean. Cool in the pans on a wire rack for 10 minutes. Then turn out onto the rack to cool to room temperature. Bring the frosting, if it has been refrigerated or frozen, to room temperature.

While the cake is baking, prepare the filling: Combine sugar, cornstarch, salt, liquid egg substitute, and water in a saucepan. Beat until smooth. Cook over medium heat, stirring constantly, until smooth and thick and the starchy taste is gone. Remove from the heat, add margarine and lemon juice, and cool to room temperature.

Spread the cooled filling between the layers of cake. Then frost the cake with the Lemon Buttercream Frosting.

NUTRITIVE VALUES PER SERVING

Number of servings 16

---

calories 233 • carbohydrate 39 grams • protein 2 grams • fat 8 grams
sodium 224 milligrams • cholesterol 0 milligrams

Low-sodium diets: Omit salt.
Use salt-free margarine and low-sodium baking powder.

SACHER TORTE

This elegant cake was the specialty of The Sacher restaurant in Vienna during the nineteenth century. The combination of apricots and chocolate is still an Austrian favorite.

YIELD: THREE 9-INCH LAYERS

1 cup apricot jam

1 cup sugar

1 cup cocoa

$^{1}/_{2}$ cup vegetable oil

$^{1}/_{4}$ teaspoon salt

$^{1}/_{2}$ cup water, at room temperature

$^{1}/_{4}$ cup egg whites or liquid egg substitute

2 teaspoons vanilla extract

2 teaspoons baking soda

$1^{1}/_{2}$ cups warm water

$2^{1}/_{4}$ cups all-purpose flour

1 cup Chocolate Powdered Sugar Frosting (page 192)

Preheat oven to 350°F. Grease and flour three 9-inch layer cake pans and set aside.

Puree apricot jam using a blender or food processor, or chop any large pieces of apricots by hand and stir the jam with a spoon to make it easier to spread. Set aside.

Place sugar, cocoa, oil, salt, and $^{1}/_{2}$ cup water in the bowl of an electric mixer and mix at medium speed until smooth and shiny. Add egg whites or liquid egg substitute and vanilla and mix at medium speed to blend, scraping down the bowl before and after the addition.

Dissolve the baking soda in $1^{1}/_{2}$ cups warm water and add, along with the flour, to the egg mixture. Mix at medium speed for 1 minute.

Pour one-third of the batter into each of the prepared pans. Bake for 30 to 35 minutes or until a cake tester inserted in the center of each layer comes out clean. Cool in the pans on a wire rack for 10 minutes. Then turn the layers out onto the rack and cool to room temperature.

Spread one of the layers with 1/2 cup apricot jam. Place another cake layer on top. Spread this with the remaining 1/2 cup jam, then top with the third cake layer. Frost the top and sides of the cake with the Chocolate Powdered Sugar Frosting.

NUTRITIVE VALUES PER SERVING

Number of servings 16

---

calories 305 • carbohydrate 56 grams • protein 3 grams • fat 9 grams
sodium 145 milligrams • cholesterol 0 milligrams

Low-sodium diets: Omit salt
and use salt-free margarine in the frosting.

PEACH UPSIDE-DOWN CAKE

This traditional cake is best served warm. If I can't serve it as soon as it is baked, I pop each piece in the microwave for a few seconds before serving it.

YIELD: ONE 9-INCH LAYER

7 tablespoons margarine, softened

1/3 cup dark brown sugar

3/4 cup sugar

1 teaspoon vanilla extract

1/2 teaspoon almond extract

1/3 cup egg whites or liquid egg substitute

1 2/3 cups all-purpose flour

2 tablespoons instant nonfat dry milk

1 1/2 teaspoons baking powder

1/4 teaspoon salt

3/4 cup water, at room temperature

6 medium peach halves, canned in fruit juice

6 medium pitted prunes

Preheat oven to 375°F. Grease a 9-inch round layer cake pan with 1 tablespoon margarine. Sprinkle brown sugar evenly over it, place it in the preheated oven, and allow it to heat for 10 minutes or until the margarine and sugar are melted together.

Meanwhile, begin preparing the cake batter: Using an electric mixer at medium speed, cream the remaining 6 tablespoons margarine and sugar together until light and fluffy. Add flavorings and egg whites or liquid egg substitute and mix at medium speed until creamy, scraping down the bowl before and after the addition.

Stir flour, dry milk, baking powder, and salt together to blend well and add to the creamy mixture, along with the water. Mix at medium speed until smooth.

Stuff each peach half with one of the pitted prunes. Then place the stuffed peaches, prune side down, on the hot brown sugar mixture and cover evenly with the cake batter. Bake for 35 minutes or until well browned and a cake tester inserted in the center comes out clean. Let the cake rest in the pan for 5 minutes. Then turn out onto a wire rack or plate. Serve warm, if possible.

NOTE: The brown sugar coating should be ready by the time the cake batter is mixed. To achieve this, you should put the brown sugar coating in at the same time that you begin to combine the ingredients for the cake batter.

VARIATIONS

1. PINEAPPLE UPSIDE-DOWN CAKE: Substitute 6 slices pineapple canned in juice for the stuffed peaches.

2. APRICOT NUT UPSIDE-DOWN CAKE: Omit the prunes. Substitute 8 well-drained apricot halves canned in juice for the peaches. Sprinkle 1/4 cup chopped pecans over the hot brown sugar mixture before adding the apricot halves.

NUTRITIVE VALUES PER SERVING

Number of servings 9

---

calories 302 • carbohydrate 52 grams • protein 10 grams • fat 9 grams
sodium 244 milligrams • cholesterol 0 milligrams

Low-sodium diets: Omit salt.
Use salt-free margarine and low-sodium baking powder.

BANANA WALNUT FRUITCAKE

My husband loved any bread or cake made with bananas. He especially enjoyed this fruitcake, which is like a good banana bread with candied fruit in it.

YIELD: ONE BUNDT CAKE OR 10-INCH TUBE CAKE

1/2 cup (1 stick) margarine

1/2 cup sugar

1/2 cup egg whites or liquid egg substitute

1 teaspoon vanilla extract

2 medium bananas

1 cup coarsely chopped black or English walnuts

2 cups chopped candied fruit

1 3/4 cups all-purpose flour

1 teaspoon baking powder

1/2 teaspoon baking soda

1/2 teaspoon salt

1/2 teaspoon cinnamon

3 to 4 tablespoons rum

Preheat oven to 400°F, placing a pan of warm water in the bottom of the oven to add steam. When the water boils, lower the heat to 300°F. Grease a Bundt (fluted tube) or 10-inch tube pan with margarine or cooking spray, line with waxed paper, and grease again. Set aside.

Using an electric mixer at medium speed, cream margarine and sugar together until light and fluffy. Add egg whites or liquid egg substitute and vanilla and mix at medium speed for 30 seconds, scraping down the bowl before and after the addition. Slice the bananas about ¼ inch thick and add to the egg mixture, beating at medium speed until smooth. Add nuts and candied fruit and mix lightly.

Stir flour, baking powder, baking soda, salt, and cinnamon together to blend well and add to the batter. Mix at medium speed until creamy. Spread the batter evenly in the prepared pan. Bake for 1 hour and 15 minutes or until a cake tester inserted in the center comes out clean. Cool in the pan on a wire rack for 15 minutes. Then turn out onto the wire rack, remove the waxed paper, and cool to room temperature.

Puncture about 10 holes in the top of the cake with a meat fork and moisten with the rum. Wrap in aluminum foil and let stand at room temperature overnight. Then refrigerate or freeze until needed.

NOTE: Please refer to page 138 for further information on fruitcakes.

NUTRITIVE VALUES PER SERVING

Number of servings 24

---

calories 190 • carbohydrate 31 grams • protein 2 grams • fat 7 grams
sodium 129 milligrams • cholesterol 0 milligrams

Low-sodium diets: Omit salt.
Use salt-free margarine and low-sodium baking powder.

BOURBON FRUITCAKE

Most fruitcakes need to be soaked with liquor or fruit juice, but this lovely fruitcake is so moist it can be served immediately or wrapped in aluminum foil and frozen until needed. My friend Cracker Holton from Clearwater, Florida, sent me my first Bourbon Fruitcake. I enjoyed it so much that I asked her for the recipe, adjusted it for a low-cholesterol diet, and have been making it ever since.

YIELD: ONE 9 BY 5 BY 3-INCH LOAF CAKE

1 cup raisins

1 cup chopped candied cherries

1 cup coarsely chopped pecans

1/2 cup grape jelly

1/4 cup (1/2 stick) margarine

1/2 cup sugar

1/4 cup molasses

3/4 cup egg whites or liquid egg substitute

2 cups all-purpose flour

1 teaspoon baking powder

1/4 teaspoon baking soda

1/2 cup bourbon whiskey

Preheat oven to 400°F, placing a pan of warm water in the bottom of the oven to add steam. When the water boils, lower the heat to 300°F. Grease a 9 by 5 by 3-inch loaf pan (preferably non-stick) with margarine or cooking spray, line with waxed paper, and grease again. Set aside.

Stir raisins, cherries, pecans, and jelly together and set aside.

Using an electric mixer at medium speed, beat margarine, sugar, and molasses together until light and fluffy. Add egg whites or liquid egg substitute and mix at medium speed for 30 seconds, scraping down the bowl before and after the addition.

Stir flour, baking powder, and baking soda together to blend and add, along with the whiskey, to the creamy mixture. Mix until creamy. Add the fruit and nut mixture and mix at medium speed only until blended.

Spread the batter evenly in the prepared pan. Bake for 1 hour and 45 minutes or until a cake tester inserted in the center comes out clean. Cool in the pan on a wire rack for 10 minutes. Then turn out onto the rack, remove the waxed paper, and cool to room temperature. Wrap in aluminum foil and refrigerate or freeze until needed.

NOTE: Please refer to page 138 for further information on fruitcakes.

NUTRITIVE VALUES PER SERVING

Number of servings 18

---

calories 238 • carbohydrate 43 grams • protein 3 grams • fat 7 grams
sodium 66 milligrams • cholesterol 0 milligrams

Low-sodium diets: Use salt-free margarine
and low-sodium baking powder.

CHOCOLATE FRUITCAKE

Patti Dillon, our Fayette County Extension Home Economist, and I are both chocoholics and we really enjoy this cake. I didn't even know there were chocolate fruitcakes until I found this one in a newspaper article in 1983. I adapted it for our low-cholesterol diet and have been making and enjoying it ever since.

YIELD: ONE 10-INCH TUBE CAKE

1 cup coarsely chopped Brazil nuts

1 cup candied cherries, halved

1 cup diced mixed fruit

1 cup raisins

1/2 cup hot coffee

1/4 cup cocoa

1/2 cup (1 stick) margarine

1 cup brown sugar

1/2 cup egg whites or liquid egg substitute

1 teaspoon vanilla extract

2 cups all-purpose flour

1 teaspoon baking powder

1/2 teaspoon baking soda

1/2 teaspoon salt

1/4 teaspoon cinnamon

1/3 cup chocolate or chocolate cherry liqueur

Preheat oven to 400°F, placing a pan of warm water in the bottom of the oven to add steam. When the water boils, lower the heat to 300°F. Grease a 10-inch tube pan (preferably non-stick) with margarine or cooking spray, line with waxed paper, and grease again. Set aside.

Stir nuts, fruit, and raisins together and set aside. Combine coffee and cocoa, mix well, and set aside.

Using an electric mixer at medium speed, cream margarine and brown sugar together until light and fluffy. Add egg whites or liquid egg substitute and vanilla and mix at medium speed until creamy, scraping down the bowl before and after the addition.

Stir flour, baking powder, baking soda, salt, and cinnamon together and add to the creamy mixture, along with the coffee and cocoa mixture. Mix until creamy. Then stir in the fruit and nut mixture.

Spread the batter evenly in the prepared pan. Bake for 1 hour and 45 minutes or until a cake tester inserted in the center comes out clean. Cool in the pan on a wire rack for 10 minutes. Then turn out onto the rack, remove the waxed paper, and cool to room temperature.

Puncture about 15 holes in the cake with a meat fork and then soak with the chocolate liqueur. Wrap in aluminum foil and let stand at room temperature overnight. Then refrigerate or freeze until needed.

NOTE: Please refer to page 138 for further information on fruitcakes.

NUTRITIVE VALUES PER SERVING

Number of servings 24

---

calories 231 • carbohydrate 40 grams • protein 3 grams • fat 8 grams
sodium 133 milligrams • cholesterol 0 milligrams

Low-sodium diets: Omit salt.
Use salt-free margarine and low-sodium baking powder.

IRISH FRUITCAKE

I love Ireland and have been there several times. Irish food highlights fresh meat and fish, as well as wonderful fresh fruits and vegetables, without a lot of fatty sauces — I find it appealing and recommend it to anyone on a low-cholesterol diet. I even love this fruitcake with the whiskey in it. It isn't as plain as most of their food, but it certainly is delicious.

YIELD: ONE BUNDT CAKE OR 10-INCH TUBE
CAKE

1 cup raisins

1 cup diced candied fruit

1/2 cup diced candied citron

1 tablespoon molasses

1/2 cup plus 3 tablespoons Irish whiskey

1/2 cup (1 stick) margarine

3/4 cup brown sugar

3/4 cup egg whites or liquid egg substitute

2 cups all-purpose flour

1 teaspoon baking powder

1/2 teaspoon baking soda

1 teaspoon cinnamon

1/4 teaspoon nutmeg

1/4 teaspoon allspice

1 cup coarsely chopped English walnuts

Preheat oven to 400°F, placing a pan of warm water in the bottom of the oven to add steam. When the water boils, lower the heat to 300°F. Grease a Bundt (fluted tube) or 10-inch tube pan (preferably non-stick) with margarine or cooking spray, line with waxed paper, and grease again. Set aside.

Stir raisins, candied fruit, molasses, and 1/2 cup whiskey together and set aside.

Using an electric mixer at medium speed, cream margarine and brown sugar together until light and fluffy. Add egg whites or liquid egg substitute and mix at medium speed for 1 minute to blend, scraping down the bowl before and after the addition.

Stir flour, baking powder, baking soda, spices, and nuts together to blend and add to the egg mixture. Mix at medium speed until creamy. Stir in the fruit mixture.

Spread the batter evenly in the prepared pan. Bake for 1 hour and 45 minutes or until a cake tester inserted in the center comes out clean. Cool in the pan for 15 minutes. Then turn out onto a wire rack, remove the waxed paper, and cool to room temperature.

Puncture the top of the cake with a meat fork about 10 times. Sprinkle with the remaining 3 tablespoons whiskey, wrap in aluminum foil, and let stand at room temperature for 2 to 3 days. Then refrigerate or freeze until needed.

NOTE: Please refer to page 138 for further information on fruitcakes.

NUTRITIVE VALUES PER SERVING

Number of servings 24

---

calories 203 • carbohydrate 34 grams • protein 3 grams • fat 7 grams
sodium 138 milligrams • cholesterol 0 milligrams

Low-sodium diets: Omit salt.
Use salt-free margarine and low-sodium baking powder.

ORANGE FRUITCAKE

I call this my "teetotaler" cake: it is the one I make as a holiday gift for my friends who don't want anything alcoholic in their cakes. Despite the absence of alcohol, it is every bit as good as my other fruitcakes.

YIELD: ONE 9 BY 5 BY 3-INCH LOAF CAKE

CAKE

½ cup chopped candied citron

½ cup chopped candied
  pineapple

½ cup chopped candied
  cherries

½ cup chopped English walnuts

1 tablespoon grated fresh or
  finely chopped dried orange
  rind

2¼ cups all-purpose flour

2 tablespoons dry buttermilk

1 teaspoon baking soda

½ teaspoon salt

½ cup (1 stick) margarine

½ cup sugar

1 teaspoon orange extract

½ cup egg whites or liquid egg
  substitute

⅔ cup water, at room
  temperature

ORANGE SYRUP

½ cup orange juice

½ cup sugar

Preheat oven to 400°F, placing a pan of warm water in the bottom of the oven to add steam. When the water boils, lower the heat to 350°F.

Grease a 9 by 5 by 3-inch loaf pan (preferably non-stick) with margarine or cooking spray, line with waxed paper, and grease again. Set aside.

Mix candied fruit, nuts, and orange rind together and set aside.

Stir flour, dry buttermilk, baking soda, and salt together to blend well. Set aside.

Using an electric mixer at medium speed, cream margarine, sugar, and orange extract together until light and fluffy. Add egg whites or liquid egg substitute and beat 1 minute at medium speed, scraping down the bowl before and after the addition. Add the flour mixture to the creamed mixture, along with the water, and mix at medium speed until creamy. Add the fruit and nut mixture and mix only to blend.

Spread the batter evenly in the prepared pan. Bake for 1 hour and 10 minutes or until the cake is lightly browned and a cake tester inserted in the center comes out clean. Cool in the pan on a wire rack.

While the cake is cooling, prepare the Orange Syrup: Combine orange juice and sugar in a saucepan. Cook over low heat, stirring until the sugar is dissolved. Remove from the heat.

Puncture about 12 holes in the top of the fruitcake with a meat fork. Then pour the hot syrup over the warm cake. Let stand for 1 hour or until completely cool. Turn the cake out of the pan, remove the waxed paper, and wrap in aluminum foil. Refrigerate and use within a few days or freeze until needed.

NOTE: Please refer to page 138 for further information on fruitcakes.

VARIATION

GRAND MARNIER FRUITCAKE: Omit the Orange Syrup. Turn the cake out of the pan after cooling for 10 minutes, remove the waxed paper, and soak the cake with 3 or 4 tablespoons Grand Marnier liqueur. Wrap in aluminum foil and let stand at room temperature overnight. Refrigerate or freeze until needed.

NUTRITIVE VALUES PER SERVING

Number of servings 18

---

calories 171 • carbohydrate 35 grams • protein 3 grams • fat 2 grams
sodium 119 milligrams • cholesterol 0 milligrams

Low-sodium diets: Omit salt
and use salt-free margarine.

REGENIA'S FRUITCAKE

This is a versatile fruitcake. You can use different kinds of fruits and nuts as long as you keep the total amounts of fruits and nuts the same. I never chop the fruit or nuts because the whole ones look so pretty when the cake is sliced. I generally freeze this cake and keep it for very special occasions.

YIELD: ONE 9 BY 5 BY 3-INCH LOAF CAKE

4 ounces (³/₄ cup) whole pitted dates

6 ounces (1 cup packed) seedless golden raisins

4 ounces (¹/₂ cup) red candied cherries

4 ounces (¹/₂ cup) green candied cherries

4 ounces (1 cup) pecan halves

4 ounces (1 cup) English walnut halves

1¹/₄ cups sugar

1³/₄ cups all-purpose flour

²/₃ cup egg whites or liquid egg substitute

1 teaspoon vanilla

1 teaspoon baking powder

¹/₂ cup light rum, brandy, or pineapple juice, divided

Preheat oven to 400°F, placing a pan of warm water in the bottom of the oven to add steam. When the water boils, lower the heat to 300°F. Grease a 9 by 5 by 3-inch loaf pan (preferably non-stick) with margarine or cooking spray, line with waxed paper, and grease again. Set aside.

Place fruit and nuts in a bowl. Add ¼ cup sugar and ¼ cup flour and mix to cover the fruit and nuts with the flour and sugar. Set aside.

Place egg whites or liquid egg substitute, remaining 1 cup sugar, and vanilla in the bowl of an electric mixer and mix at medium speed to blend. Stir remaining 1½ cups flour and baking powder together to blend and add to the egg mixture, along with ¼ cup rum, brandy, or juice. Mix at medium speed to blend and pour over the fruit and nut mixture. Stir to blend.

Spread the batter evenly in the prepared pan. Bake for 1 hour and 45 minutes to 2 hours or until the cake is browned and a cake tester inserted in the center comes out clean. Cool in the pan on a wire rack for 10 minutes. Then turn out onto the rack, remove the waxed paper, and cool to room temperature.

Puncture 10 holes in the cake with a meat fork and soak with the remaining ¼ cup rum, brandy, or juice. Wrap in aluminum foil and let stand at room temperature overnight. Refrigerate or freeze until needed.

NOTE: Please refer to page 138 for further information on fruitcakes.

NUTRITIVE VALUES PER SERVING

Number of servings 24

---

calories 221 • carbohydrate 36 grams • protein 3 grams • fat 7 grams
sodium 24 milligrams • cholesterol 0 milligrams

Low-sodium diets: Recipe may be used as written.

COFFEE
CAKES

APPLE COFFEE CAKE

BANANA BREAKFAST COFFEE CAKE

BRAN NUT COFFEE CAKE

CINNAMON PECAN COFFEE CAKE

DATE BRAN COFFEE CAKE

RAISIN BRAN COFFEE CAKE

SCHNECKEN

SPECIAL COFFEE CAKE

SPECIAL PECAN COFFEE CAKE

SPECIAL RAISIN COFFEE CAKE

SPECIAL CANDIED FRUIT COFFEE CAKE

WHOLE-WHEAT CINNAMON ROLLS

COFFEE CAKES DON'T have to be reserved for breakfast. You can serve them whenever you like — for dessert, as an afternoon treat, or at a coffee party. All you need is coffee cake, good hot coffee, friends, and some time to enjoy them.

Most coffee cakes are of European origin. Scandinavians are famous for their wonderful coffee cakes and Italians for their Panettone. And who can forget the elaborate beauties served with coffee in Vienna. Americans have adopted all of these wonderful coffee cakes and added many of their own.

Coffee cakes are generally either yeast breads or quick breads made with baking soda or baking powder for leavening. Both kinds are often enriched with fruits, dates, raisins, nuts, frostings, and spices. The dough for either type can be very rich or very lean, depending upon the occasion and your own needs. My family can't afford to eat very rich doughs on our low-fat, low-sugar, low-cholesterol diet, but we still like tasty and interesting coffee cakes. Fortunately, I've been able to reach a happy medium with the delicious low-fat, low-sugar, cholesterol-free coffee cakes that follow in this chapter. I have added fiber to some of the coffee cakes because I know that an increased amount of fiber can help lower your cholesterol count.

Generally the basic rules provided in Cake Preparation (page 5) apply to coffee cakes also. There is this difference, however. Yeast breads and quick breads prepared with baking soda or baking powder should be mixed, baked, and served as soon as possible. Never overmix them and never let them sit before you bake them unless you are directed to do so by the recipe.

APPLE COFFEE CAKE

The first time I tasted this coffee cake was on a warm October day, when a friend's grandmother served it to us out on her back porch. I like to remember that glorious day by making this coffee cake every year with some of the first fall apples.

YIELD: ONE 9-INCH SQUARE CAKE

TOPPING

¼ **cup sugar**
1 **teaspoon cinnamon**
1 **tablespoon margarine**
¼ **cup chopped pecans**

CAKE

1 **cup all-purpose flour**
1 **cup rolled oats**
2 **tablespoons instant nonfat dry milk**

⅓ **cup sugar**
1 **tablespoon baking powder**
¼ **teaspoon salt**
¼ **cup egg whites or liquid egg substitute**
¼ **cup vegetable oil**
½ **cup water, at room temperature**
1½ **cups cored and coarsely chopped crisp apples (2 medium)**

Preheat oven to 375°F. Grease a 9-inch square cake pan with margarine or cooking spray and set aside.

Prepare the topping: Blend sugar, cinnamon, margarine, and pecans together and set aside.

Place flour, oatmeal, dry milk, sugar, baking powder, and salt in the bowl of an electric mixer and mix at low speed for 30 seconds to blend. Stir egg whites or liquid egg substitute, oil, and water together with a fork and add to the flour mixture. Mix only until the flour is moistened.

Spread half of the batter in the prepared pan. Arrange the apples evenly over the batter, cover with the rest of the batter, and then sprinkle the topping evenly over the batter. Bake for 30 to 40 minutes or until browned and firm. Serve warm.

NUTRITIVE VALUES PER SERVING

Number of servings 12

---

calories 190 • carbohydrate 26 grams • protein 3 grams • fat 8 grams
sodium 161 milligrams • cholesterol 0 milligrams

Low-sodium diets: Omit salt.
Use salt-free margarine and low-sodium baking powder.

BANANA BREAKFAST COFFEE CAKE

YIELD: ONE 9-INCH SQUARE CAKE

TOPPING

¼ cup brown sugar

2 tablespoons margarine

¼ cup chopped black or
English walnuts

CAKE

½ cup sugar

6 tablespoons (¾ stick)
margarine

1 teaspoon vanilla extract

¼ cup egg whites or liquid egg
substitute

1 tablespoon lemon juice

2 medium bananas

2 cups all-purpose flour

1 teaspoon baking soda

¼ teaspoon salt

Preheat oven to 375°F. Grease a 9-inch square cake pan with margarine or cooking spray and set aside.

Prepare the topping: Blend brown sugar, margarine, and nuts together and set aside.

Using an electric mixer at medium speed, cream sugar, margarine, and vanilla together until light and fluffy. Add egg whites or liquid egg substitute and lemon juice and mix at medium speed for 30 seconds, scraping down the bowl before and after the addition.

Slice the bananas ¼ inch thick, add to the egg mixture, and mix at medium speed for 1 minute. Stir flour, baking soda, and salt together to blend and add to the banana mixture. Mix at medium speed to blend.

Spread the batter evenly in the prepared pan. Sprinkle the topping evenly over the batter and pat it down with the back of a tablespoon. Bake for 30 minutes or until lightly browned and a cake tester inserted in the center comes out clean. Serve warm or at room temperature.

NUTRITIVE VALUES PER SERVING

Number of servings 16

---

calories 171 • carbohydrate 25 grams • protein 3 grams • fat 7 grams
sodium 159 milligrams • cholesterol 0 milligrams

Low-sodium diets: Omit salt
and use salt-free margarine.

BRAN NUT COFFEE CAKE

YIELD: ONE 11 BY 15-INCH CAKE

TOPPING

1/3 cup brown sugar

2 tablespoons margarine

1 teaspoon cinnamon

1/4 cup chopped pecans

CAKE

1 cup All Bran, Bran Buds, 100% Bran, or Fiber One cereal

1 cup water

1/2 cup (1 stick) margarine

3/4 cup sugar

1 1/2 teaspoons vanilla extract

1/2 cup egg whites or liquid egg substitute

2 cups all-purpose flour

2 tablespoons instant nonfat dry milk

1 tablespoon baking powder

1/2 teaspoon salt

1 teaspoon cinnamon

Preheat oven to 375°F. Grease an 11 by 15-inch jelly roll pan with margarine or cooking spray and set aside.

Prepare topping: Blend brown sugar, margarine, cinnamon, and pecans together and set aside.

Stir bran cereal and water together and set aside.

Using an electric mixer at medium speed, cream margarine and sugar together until light and fluffy. Add vanilla and egg whites or liquid egg substitute and mix at medium speed until creamy, scraping down the bowl before and after the addition.

Stir flour, dry milk, baking powder, salt, and cinnamon together to blend well and add to the egg mixture, along with the cereal and water mixture. Mix at medium speed until all of the flour is moistened.

Spread the batter evenly in the prepared pan. Sprinkle the topping evenly over the batter and bake for 20 to 25 minutes or until browned and firm. Serve warm.

NUTRITIVE VALUES PER SERVING

Number of servings 20

---

calories 163 • carbohydrate 24 grams • protein 3 grams • fat 7 grams
sodium 231 milligrams • cholesterol 0 milligrams

Low-sodium diets: Omit salt.
Use salt-free margarine and low-sodium baking powder.

CINNAMON PECAN COFFEE CAKE

This basic coffee cake recipe can be made several ways: Omit the topping and add dates, nuts, or raisins to the batter. Swirl the topping through the batter instead of layering, or use any of the other toppings in this chapter. The batter can also be baked in a 9-inch square cake pan or made into 16 cupcakes.

YIELD: ONE 9 BY 5 BY 3-INCH LOAF CAKE OR ONE 9-INCH SQUARE CAKE OR 16 CUPCAKES

TOPPING

1/4 cup brown sugar

1/4 cup chopped pecans

1 teaspoon cinnamon

1/2 teaspoon vanilla extract

CAKE

1/2 cup (1 stick) margarine

1/2 cup sugar

1/2 cup liquid egg substitute

1 teaspoon vanilla extract

2 1/2 cups all-purpose flour

1/4 cup dry buttermilk

1 teaspoon baking powder

1 teaspoon baking soda

1/2 teaspoon salt

2/3 cup water, at room temperature

Preheat oven to 350°F. Grease a 9 by 5 by 3-inch loaf pan with margarine or cooking spray and set aside.

Prepare the topping: Combine brown sugar, pecans, cinnamon, and vanilla. Mix well and set aside.

Using an electric mixer at medium speed, cream margarine and sugar together until light and fluffy. Add liquid egg substitute and vanilla and mix at medium speed for 30 seconds, scraping down the bowl before and after the addition.

Stir flour, dry buttermilk, baking powder, baking soda, and salt together to blend well and add to the egg mixture, along with the water. Mix at medium speed until creamy. Spread half of the batter evenly in the prepared pan. Sprinkle half of the topping evenly over the batter and spread the rest of the batter over the topping. Sprinkle the remaining topping on top of the batter. Bake for 50 minutes or until browned and a cake tester inserted in the center comes out clean. Cool in the pan on a wire rack for 10 minutes. Then turn out onto the rack. Serve warm or at room temperature.

NUTRITIVE VALUES PER SERVING

Number of servings 16

---

calories 181 • carbohydrate 26 grams • protein 3 grams • fat 7 grams
sodium 227 milligrams • cholesterol 1 milligram

Low-sodium diets: Omit salt.
Use salt-free margarine and low-sodium baking powder.

DATE BRAN COFFEE CAKE

Any of the bran cereals called for below is suitable for this coffee cake. I generally use All Bran, but I have tried all of them and they are all successful.

YIELD: ONE 9-INCH SQUARE CAKE

1½ cups all-purpose flour

1½ cups Bran Buds, 100% Bran, All Bran, or Fiber One cereal

½ cup brown sugar

½ cup chopped, pitted dates

2 tablespoons instant nonfat dry milk

1 teaspoon baking powder

1 teaspoon baking soda

¼ teaspoon salt

1½ cups water, at room temperature

⅓ cup vegetable oil

⅓ cup molasses

¼ cup egg whites or liquid egg substitute

Preheat oven to 350°F. Grease a 9-inch square cake pan with margarine or cooking spray and set aside.

Place flour, bran cereal, brown sugar, dates, dry milk, baking powder, baking soda, and salt in the bowl of an electric mixer and mix at low speed to blend well. Beat water, oil, molasses, and egg whites or liquid egg substitute together to blend well and add to flour mixture. Mix at medium speed until creamy.

Pour the batter into the prepared pan. Bake for 40 minutes or until the coffee cake pulls away from the sides of the pan and a cake tester inserted in the center comes out clean. Serve warm.

VARIATION

RAISIN BRAN COFFEE CAKE: Omit dates and add ½ cup raisins.

NUTRITIVE VALUES PER SERVING

Number of servings 16

---

calories 161 • carbohydrate 29 grams • protein 3 grams • fat 5 grams
sodium 207 milligrams • cholesterol 0 milligrams

Low-sodium diets: Omit salt
and use low-sodium baking powder.

SCHNECKEN

These rich, gooey rolls are a special Pennsylvania Dutch treat and a delicious accompaniment for coffee.

YIELD: 12 ROLLS

FILLING

1/2 cup brown sugar

1 teaspoon cinnamon

3 tablespoons margarine

1/4 cup chopped pecans

1/4 cup raisins

CAKE

2 tablespoons sugar

2 tablespoons instant nonfat
dry milk

2 tablespoons instant potato
flakes or buds

1 packet (2 1/4 teaspoons) quick-
rising active dry yeast

1 1/2 cups water, at 100° to 115°F

3 cups bread flour

2 tablespoons margarine

1 teaspoon salt

Prepare the filling: Blend brown sugar, cinnamon, and margarine together and set aside. In a separate container, mix together the pecans and raisins and set aside.

Place sugar, dry milk, instant potatoes, and yeast in the bowl of an electric mixer. Mix lightly, add water, and mix again just to combine.

Add 2 cups bread flour and mix, using a dough hook attachment, at medium speed for 4 minutes. Add margarine, salt, and remaining 1 cup bread flour and mix for another 4 minutes at medium speed. Turn the dough out onto a floured working surface and knead lightly until soft and elastic. Form into a ball and place in a bowl that has been greased with margarine. Turn the ball over to grease the top, cover with a clean cloth, and let rise at room temperature until doubled in volume.

While the dough is rising, grease a 12-cup muffin tin with margarine or cooking spray, or line with aluminum foil or silicone-treated paper liners. (Do not use untreated liners.) Place 1 teaspoon of the filling in the bottom of each cup. Add the nut and raisin mixture to the remaining filling and set aside.

When the dough is doubled in volume, turn it out onto a floured working surface, knead lightly, form into a ball, cover, and let rest for 10 minutes. Roll the ball out on a floured working surface to form a 9 by 12-inch rectangle. Spread the remaining filling evenly over the dough, leaving a 1/4-inch border without any topping. Roll lengthwise into a 12-inch-long cylinder and cut into 12 even slices, each 1 inch wide.

Place a roll, cut side down, in each of the prepared muffin cups. Cover and let rise until doubled in volume. Bake in a preheated 375°F oven for 20 to 25 minutes or until browned and firm. Turn out of the pans as soon as possible and remove the papers immediately, if necessary. Serve warm.

NUTRITIVE VALUES PER SERVING

Number of servings 12

---

calories 199 • carbohydrate 35 grams • protein 3 grams • fat 5 grams
sodium 257 milligrams • cholesterol 0 milligrams

Low-sodium diets: Omit salt
and use salt-free margarine.

SPECIAL COFFEE CAKE

This is generally called Sour Cream Coffee Cake, but when I took out the sour cream, I changed its name.

YIELD: ONE 10-INCH TUBE CAKE OR ONE BUNDT CAKE

TOPPING

½ cup chopped pecans

2 tablespoons brown sugar

½ teaspoon cinnamon

CAKE

½ cup (1 stick) margarine

1 cup sugar

¼ cup liquid egg substitute

1 teaspoon vanilla extract

2 cups all-purpose flour

2 tablespoons instant nonfat
  dry milk

1 teaspoon baking powder

1 teaspoon baking soda

1 tablespoon lemon juice

⅔ cup water, at room
  temperature

Preheat oven to 350°F. Grease a 10-inch tube or Bundt (fluted tube) pan with margarine or cooking spray and set aside.

Prepare the topping: Mix pecans, brown sugar, and cinnamon together and set aside.

Using an electric mixer at medium speed, cream margarine and sugar together until light and fluffy. Add liquid egg substitute and vanilla and mix at medium speed until creamy, scraping down the bowl before and after the addition.

Stir flour, dry milk, baking powder, and baking soda together to blend and add, along with the lemon juice and water, to the creamy mixture. Mix at medium speed for 1 minute.

Spread the batter evenly in the prepared pan and sprinkle with the reserved topping. Bake for 45 minutes or until the cake pulls away from the sides of the pan and a cake tester inserted in the center comes out clean. Cool in the pan on a wire rack for 10 minutes. Then turn out onto the rack and cool to room temperature.

NOTE: Egg whites may be used instead of liquid egg substitute, but the cake will be white instead of the characteristic yellow.

VARIATIONS

1. SPECIAL PECAN COFFEE CAKE: Omit the topping. Add 1 teaspoon cinnamon and ¾ cup chopped pecans to the batter, along with the flour mixture.

2. SPECIAL RAISIN COFFEE CAKE: Omit the topping. Add ¾ cup raisins to the batter, along with the flour mixture.

3. SPECIAL CANDIED FRUIT COFFEE CAKE: Omit the topping. Add ½ cup chopped candied fruit to the batter, along with the flour mixture.

NUTRITIVE VALUES PER SERVING

Number of servings 16

---

calories 189 • carbohydrate 28 grams • protein 3 grams • fat 8 grams
sodium 149 milligrams • cholesterol 0 milligrams

Low-sodium diets: Use salt-free margarine
and low-sodium baking powder.

WHOLE-WHEAT
CINNAMON ROLLS

Cinnamon rolls are one of the "comfort foods" in my family. My mother almost always made them when she baked bread, which was at least once a week, since my father thought "boughten" bread wasn't good for you. However, she made them from white flour and I make them from whole-wheat flour, which I think is healthier.

YIELD: 16 ROLLS

1 tablespoon plus 2 teaspoons margarine, softened

6 tablespoons sugar

1¹/₂ teaspoons cinnamon

1 packet (2¹/₄ teaspoons) quick-rising active dry yeast

1 cup water, at 110° to 115°F

1¹/₂ cups bread flour

¹/₂ teaspoon salt

¹/₈ teaspoon ground ginger

2 tablespoons vegetable oil

¹/₃ cup egg whites or liquid egg substitute

1 cup whole-wheat flour

Grease an 11 by 15-inch jelly roll pan with 2 teaspoons margarine and set aside. Stir 4 tablespoons sugar and ¹/₂ teaspoon cinnamon together to blend well and set aside.

Stir yeast and remaining 2 tablespoons sugar together in the bowl of an electric mixer. Add water and let stand for 5 minutes or until bubbly. Add bread flour and beat at medium speed, using a dough hook, for 4 minutes. Add salt, ginger, remaining 1 teaspoon cinnamon, oil, egg whites or liquid egg substitute, and whole-wheat flour in that order and beat at medium speed for another 4 minutes.

Turn the dough out onto a lightly floured surface and knead to form a ball. Place the ball in a bowl that has been greased with margarine, turning the ball over to grease the top of it. Cover and let stand at room temperature until doubled in volume.

Turn the dough out again onto a lightly floured surface and roll out to form a 9 by 12-inch rectangle. Spread the dough evenly with the remaining 1 tablespoon margarine. Sprinkle evenly with the reserved cinnamon and sugar mixture and roll like a jelly roll to form a roll 12 inches long. Cut the roll crosswise into 16 even slices, each about 3/4 inch thick. Place the slices on a greased jelly roll pan. Cover and let rise until doubled in volume.

Bake in a preheated 375°F oven for 20 to 25 minutes or until lightly browned and firm. Turn out immediately onto a wire rack and serve warm, if possible. The rolls may be glazed with Powdered Sugar Glaze (page 193), although the glaze is not included in the nutritive information.

NUTRITIVE VALUES PER SERVING

Number of servings 16

---

calories 118 • carbohydrate 21 grams • protein 3 grams • fat 3 grams
sodium 84 milligrams • cholesterol 0 milligrams

Low-sodium diets: Omit salt
and use salt-free margarine.

FROSTINGS
AND SAUCES

CHOCOLATE FUDGE FROSTING
CHOCOLATE FUDGE NUT FROSTING
CHOCOLATE FUDGE RUM FROSTING
CHOCOLATE PEPPERMINT FUDGE FROSTING
ALMOND FUDGE FROSTING
ALMOND NUT FUDGE FROSTING
PEPPERMINT FUDGE FROSTING
LEMON FUDGE FROSTING
VANILLA FUDGE FROSTING
CREAMY FROSTING
CREAMY LEMON FROSTING
CREAMY ORANGE FROSTING
MAPLE SYRUP FROSTING
WHITE MOUNTAIN FROSTING
MAPLE MOUNTAIN FROSTING
PEPPERMINT MOUNTAIN FROSTING
LEMON MOUNTAIN FROSTING
VANILLA BUTTERCREAM FROSTING
CHOCOLATE BUTTERCREAM FROSTING
CHOCOLATE RUM BUTTERCREAM FROSTING
MOCHA BUTTERCREAM FROSTING
ORANGE BUTTERCREAM FROSTING
LEMON BUTTERCREAM FROSTING

PEPPERMINT BUTTERCREAM FROSTING

VANILLA POWDERED SUGAR FROSTING

CHOCOLATE POWDERED SUGAR FROSTING

CHOCOLATE PEPPERMINT POWDERED SUGAR FROSTING

LEMON POWDERED SUGAR FROSTING

ORANGE POWDERED SUGAR FROSTING

POWDERED SUGAR GLAZE

LEMON GLAZE

ITALIAN MERINGUE

WHIPPED TOPPING

CHOCOLATE SAUCE

SWEET CHOCOLATE SAUCE

LIGHT CHOCOLATE SAUCE

SEMISWEET CHOCOLATE SAUCE

CHOCOLATE PEANUT BUTTER SAUCE

CHOCOLATE NUT SAUCE

CHOCOLATE CHERRY SAUCE

CHOCOLATE PEPPERMINT SAUCE

CHOCOLATE RUM SAUCE

CUSTARD SAUCE

RUM CUSTARD SAUCE

LEMON SAUCE

ORANGE SAUCE

I'M SURE YOU will agree that many frostings and sauces are too high in fat and sugar to be used very often. I have lowered the fat content as much as possible in each of these recipes and the sugar content whenever possible, but most of the recipes still contain too much fat and sugar for casual use. For general use, I recommend Creamy Frosting (page 185) and White Mountain Frosting (page 188), both of which are lower in sugar than the other frostings in this chapter. The White Mountain Frosting also happens to be fat-free. I have reduced the fat content in the Vanilla Buttercream Frosting and the Vanilla Powdered Sugar Frosting, but I wasn't able to reduce the sugar content by much because it takes a certain amount of powdered sugar to achieve the right consistency. Besides, if you cut the amount of sugar by much, you'll find yourself with a lot of cake and not enough frosting to cover it.

If you want to dress up a plain cake without loading it with a lot of frosting, you should try topping it with any of the toppings or sauces in this chapter. Whipped Topping (page 196) and Italian Meringue (page 195) are delicious and add a lot to a plain cake or pudding, as does Chocolate Sauce (page 198).

The frostings and sauces in this chapter are easy to make, but three of them require a candy thermometer—White Mountain Frosting, Italian Meringue, and Maple Syrup Frosting (page 187). These recipes incorporate a sugar syrup, and the temperature of this syrup is very important. You won't get good results unless you cook the sugar syrup to the right temperature: If the syrup is undercooked, the frosting or sauce will be too soft; if the syrup is overcooked, the frosting or sauce will turn to candy. You must remember to watch that thermometer.

Powdered sugar is called confectioners' sugar in many areas of the country. You will get the same good results whether you buy powdered or confectioners' sugar.

CHOCOLATE FUDGE FROSTING

You'll get a nice, glossy finish if you spread this frosting while it is still warm. It will spread when it is cool, but it loses its sheen. Its fudgy taste adds the perfect touch to a chocolate or white cake.

YIELD: TWO AND A QUARTER CUPS

¼ cup (½ stick) margarine, softened

1 pound (4 cups) powdered or confectioners' sugar

¼ teaspoon salt

½ cup cocoa

1½ teaspoons vanilla extract

¼ cup light corn syrup

3 tablespoons water

Place margarine, powdered sugar, salt, cocoa, and vanilla in the bowl of an electric mixer and mix at low speed for 30 seconds to blend well.

Combine corn syrup and water in a small saucepan and bring to a simmer. (Do not boil.) Add the hot syrup all at once to the powdered sugar mixture and beat at medium speed for 1 minute or until smooth and well blended. Spread on a cooled cake while the frosting is still warm.

NOTE: This frosting should always be spread on the cake while the frosting is warm, since it loses its gloss when it is cooled. This frosting may be refrigerated or frozen until needed, but it should be reheated in a microwave oven or double boiler before it is used.

VARIATIONS

1. CHOCOLATE FUDGE NUT FROSTING: Add 1 cup chopped nuts to the finished frosting.

2. CHOCOLATE FUDGE RUM FROSTING: Use 1½ teaspoons rum flavoring instead of the vanilla.

3. CHOCOLATE PEPPERMINT FUDGE FROSTING: Use 1 teaspoon peppermint flavoring instead of the vanilla.

NUTRITIVE VALUES FOR TOTAL RECIPE

calories 2,290 • carbohydrate 486 grams • protein 8 grams • fat 52 grams
sodium 1,125 milligrams • cholesterol 0 milligrams

Low-sodium diets: Omit salt
and use salt-free margarine.

NUTRITIVE VALUES PER TABLESPOON

Number of servings 36

calories 64 • carbohydrate 13 grams • protein 0 grams • fat 1 gram
sodium 31 milligrams • cholesterol 0 milligrams

Low-sodium diets: Omit salt
and use salt-free margarine.

ALMOND FUDGE FROSTING

You'll love this frosting. It tastes like a good almond fudge — creamy yet firm. It keeps well in the refrigerator or freezer, so you can prepare your cake for a special occasion days in advance.

YIELD: TWO AND A QUARTER CUPS

1 pound (4 cups) powdered or confectioners' sugar

1/3 cup all-purpose flour

1/4 teaspoon salt

6 tablespoons (3/4 stick) margarine

1/4 cup light corn syrup

1/4 cup water

2 teaspoons almond extract

Stir powdered sugar, flour, and salt together to blend well. Set aside. Combine margarine, syrup, and water in a 2-quart saucepan. Cook over low heat, stirring, until margarine is melted. Add sugar mixture and continue to cook over low heat, stirring, until smooth and shiny. Remove from heat, add almond extract, and frost cake immediately.

NOTE: This frosting should always be spread on the cake while the frosting is still warm, since it loses its gloss when it is cooled. This frosting may be refrigerated or frozen until needed, but it should be reheated in a micro-wave oven or double boiler before it is used.

VARIATIONS

1. ALMOND NUT FUDGE FROSTING: Add 1/2 cup chopped nuts to the finished frosting.

2. PEPPERMINT FUDGE FROSTING: Omit almond extract and add 1 teaspoon peppermint flavoring and 2 or 3 drops red or green food coloring.

3. LEMON FUDGE FROSTING: Omit almond extract and add 2 teaspoons lemon extract and 2 or 3 drops yellow food coloring.

4. VANILLA FUDGE FROSTING: Omit almond extract and add 1 table-spoon vanilla extract.

NUTRITIVE VALUES FOR TOTAL RECIPE

calories 2,542 • carbohydrate 494 grams • protein 4 grams • fat 69 grams
sodium 433 milligrams • cholesterol 0 milligrams

Low-sodium diets: Omit salt
and use salt-free margarine.

NUTRITIVE VALUES PER TABLESPOON

Number of servings 36

calories 71 • carbohydrate 14 grams • protein 0 grams • fat 2 grams
sodium 40 milligrams • cholesterol 0 milligrams

Low-sodium diets: Omit salt
and use salt-free margarine.

CREAMY FROSTING

Because the flavor can be varied, this light and luscious frosting is good with just about any cake.

YIELD: TWO CUPS

¼ cup all-purpose flour
¼ cup instant nonfat dry milk
1 cup cold water
½ cup (1 stick) margarine

1 cup powdered or
confectioners' sugar
1½ teaspoons vanilla extract

Combine flour, dry milk, and water in a small saucepan. Mix until smooth and then cook over medium heat, stirring constantly, until thickened. Continue to cook, stirring, for another 30 seconds. Cool to room temperature.

While the flour mixture is cooling, use an electric mixer at medium speed to cream the margarine until light and fluffy. Then gradually beat the flour mixture into the margarine. Add the powdered sugar and vanilla and beat at medium speed for 5 minutes.

VARIATIONS

1. CREAMY LEMON FROSTING: Substitute 1½ teaspoons lemon extract for the vanilla.

2. CREAMY ORANGE FROSTING: Substitute 1½ teaspoons orange extract for the vanilla.

NUTRITIVE VALUES FOR TOTAL RECIPE

calories 1,371 • carbohydrate 133 grams • protein 9 grams • fat 92 grams
sodium 1,214 milligrams • cholesterol 4 milligrams

Low-sodium diets: Use salt-free margarine.

NUTRITIVE VALUES PER TABLESPOON

Number of servings 32

calories 43 • carbohydrate 4 grams • protein trace • fat 3 grams
sodium 38 milligrams • cholesterol 0 milligrams

Low-sodium diets: Use salt-free margarine.

MAPLE SYRUP FROSTING

YIELD: ONE AND A HALF CUPS

³/₄ cup maple syrup

¹/₄ cup water

1 egg white, at room
temperature

¹/₈ teaspoon salt

¹/₄ teaspoon cream of tartar

¹/₄ cup sugar

1 teaspoon maple flavoring

Combine maple syrup and water in a small saucepan and cook over medium heat until the mixture registers 238°F on a candy thermometer. This temperature is very important. If it is lower the frosting will be too soft, and if it is higher the mixture will have the consistency of candy instead of frosting.

While the syrup is cooking, combine the egg white, salt, and cream of tartar in the bowl of an electric mixer. Using a whip attachment, beat the egg white mixture at high speed until foamy. Add the sugar gradually, while beating at high speed. Continue beating until the egg white mixture is glossy and stiff. With the mixer still running, add the flavoring. Then gradually add the hot syrup. Beat at medium speed until cool. Use immediately. Do not freeze.

NUTRITIVE VALUES FOR TOTAL RECIPE

calories 813 • carbohydrate 204 grams • protein 0 grams • fat 0 grams
sodium 267 milligrams • cholesterol 0 milligrams

Low-sodium diets: Omit salt.

NUTRITIVE VALUES PER TABLESPOON

Number of servings 24

---

calories 34 • carbohydrate 9 grams • protein 0 grams • fat 0 grams
sodium 11 milligrams • cholesterol 0 milligrams

Low-sodium diets: Omit salt.

WHITE MOUNTAIN FROSTING

This frosting doesn't freeze well, but it is so light and delicious that I use it often. It is fat-free, too, which is a big plus for everyone.

YIELD: THREE CUPS

1 cup sugar

1/8 teaspoon salt

1 tablespoon lemon juice

1/2 cup water

2 large egg whites, at room temperature

1 teaspoon vanilla extract

Combine sugar, salt, lemon juice, and water in a small saucepan. Cook over medium heat, stirring frequently, just until the mixture registers 235°F on a candy thermometer.

While the syrup is cooking, use an electric mixer with a whip attachment to beat the egg whites at high speed until they hold soft peaks. Add the syrup gradually, continuing to beat at high speed, until the frosting is stiff.

Stir in vanilla. Cool to room temperature before spreading. Do not freeze.

VARIATIONS

1. MAPLE MOUNTAIN FROSTING: Omit vanilla and add 1 teaspoon maple flavoring.

2. PEPPERMINT MOUNTAIN FROSTING: Omit vanilla and add 1 teaspoon peppermint flavoring and 2 or 3 drops red food coloring.

3. LEMON MOUNTAIN FROSTING: Omit vanilla and add 1 teaspoon lemon extract and 2 or 3 drops yellow food coloring.

NUTRITIVE VALUES FOR TOTAL RECIPE

calories 808 • carbohydrate 201 grams • protein 7 grams • fat 0 grams
sodium 363 milligrams • cholesterol 0 milligrams

Low-sodium diets: Omit salt.

NUTRITIVE VALUES PER TABLESPOON

Number of servings 48

calories 17 • carbohydrate 4 grams • protein 0 grams • fat 0 grams
sodium 8 milligrams • cholesterol 0 milligrams

Low-sodium diets: Omit salt.

VANILLA BUTTERCREAM FROSTING

We all know there is no butter in this frosting, but "margarine-cream frosting" doesn't sound quite right, so I pretend and call it buttercream frosting.

YIELD: TWO CUPS

⅓ cup (⅔ stick) margarine, softened

1 pound (4 cups) powdered or confectioners' sugar

¼ teaspoon salt

3 tablespoons skim milk

1 teaspoon vanilla extract

Using an electric mixer at medium speed, cream margarine until light and fluffy. Add powdered sugar, salt, milk, and vanilla and beat at medium speed until smooth and creamy.

NOTE: This frosting may be refrigerated or frozen but it must be brought back to room temperature before it is used.

VARIATIONS

1. CHOCOLATE BUTTERCREAM FROSTING: Omit milk. Add ¼ cup cocoa and ¼ cup hot water.

2. CHOCOLATE RUM BUTTERCREAM FROSTING: Omit milk. Add ¼ cup cocoa, ¼ cup hot water, and 1 teaspoon rum flavoring.

3. MOCHA BUTTERCREAM FROSTING: Omit milk. Add 2 tablespoons cocoa and 3 tablespoons strong, hot coffee.

4. ORANGE BUTTERCREAM FROSTING: Omit milk and vanilla. Add 3 tablespoons orange juice and 1 teaspoon orange extract.

5. LEMON BUTTERCREAM FROSTING: Omit milk and vanilla. Add 1 tablespoon grated lemon peel and 1 teaspoon lemon extract.

6. PEPPERMINT BUTTERCREAM FROSTING: Omit vanilla. Add 1 teaspoon peppermint flavoring and 1 or 2 drops red or green food coloring.

NUTRITIVE VALUES FOR TOTAL RECIPE

calories 2,134 • carbohydrate 402 grams • protein 1 gram • fat 59 grams
sodium 1,261 milligrams • cholesterol 2 milligrams

Low-sodium diets: Omit salt
and use salt-free margarine.

NUTRITIVE VALUES PER TABLESPOON

Number of servings 32

calories 67 • carbohydrate 13 grams • protein 0 grams • fat 2 grams
sodium 39 milligrams • cholesterol 0 milligrams

Low-sodium diets: Omit salt
and use salt-free margarine.

VANILLA POWDERED SUGAR FROSTING

This simple frosting resembles Vanilla Buttercream Frosting (page 190) but contains less fat. I like to keep several flavors in the freezer to simplify cake preparation when I'm in a hurry.

YIELD: TWO CUPS

1 pound (4 cups) powdered or confectioners' sugar

2 tablespoons instant nonfat dry milk

1/4 teaspoon salt

1 1/2 teaspoons vanilla extract

1/4 cup (1/2 stick) margarine, softened

3 to 4 tablespoons water, at room temperature

Combine powdered sugar, dry milk, and salt in the bowl of an electric mixer and mix at medium speed for 30 seconds to blend well. Add vanilla, margarine, and 3 tablespoons water. Mix at medium speed until light and fluffy, adding the remaining 1 tablespoon water if necessary.

NOTE: This frosting may be refrigerated or frozen but it must be brought back to room temperature before it is used.

VARIATIONS

1. CHOCOLATE POWDERED SUGAR FROSTING: Add 2 tablespoons cocoa to the sugar mixture and use boiling water instead of water at room temperature.

2. CHOCOLATE PEPPERMINT POWDERED SUGAR FROSTING: Prepare Chocolate Powdered Sugar Frosting, substituting 1 teaspoon peppermint flavoring for the vanilla.

3. LEMON POWDERED SUGAR FROSTING: Omit vanilla. Add 1 teaspoon lemon extract, 1 tablespoon grated fresh or finely chopped dried lemon rind, and 2 or 3 drops yellow food coloring.

4. ORANGE POWDERED SUGAR FROSTING: Omit dry milk, vanilla, and water. Add 1 teaspoon orange extract and 3 or 4 tablespoons orange juice.

NUTRITIVE VALUES FOR TOTAL RECIPE

calories 1,972 • carbohydrate 405 grams • protein 3 grams • fat 44 grams
sodium 1,117 milligrams • cholesterol 2 milligrams

Low-sodium diets: Omit salt
and use salt-free margarine.

NUTRITIVE VALUES PER TABLESPOON

Number of servings 32

calories 62 • carbohydrate 13 grams • protein 0 grams • fat 1 gram
sodium 35 milligrams • cholesterol 0 milligrams

Low-sodium diets: Omit salt
and use salt-free margarine.

POWDERED SUGAR GLAZE

YIELD: THREE-QUARTER CUP

**2 cups powdered or
confectioners' sugar**

**3 tablespoons water
1 teaspoon vanilla extract**

Combine powdered sugar, water, and vanilla and stir until smooth.

NOTE: Leftover glaze should be refrigerated or frozen until needed but it should be returned to room temperature before it is used.

VARIATION

LEMON GLAZE: Substitute 3 tablespoons lemon juice for the water.

NUTRITIVE VALUES FOR TOTAL RECIPE

calories 770 • carbohydrate 200 grams • protein 0 grams • fat 0 grams
sodium 0 milligrams • cholesterol 0 milligrams

Low-sodium diets: Recipe may be used as written.

NUTRITIVE VALUES PER TABLESPOON

Number of servings 12

calories 64 • carbohydrate 16 grams • protein 0 grams • fat 0 grams
sodium 0 milligrams • cholesterol 0 milligrams

Low-sodium diets: Recipe may be used as written.

ITALIAN MERINGUE

This is soft, fat-free meringue which makes a good frosting for cakes or topping for puddings. I prefer to use it fresh but it can be refrigerated and used the next day if it is whipped again with a large spoon or wire whip.

YIELD: TWO QUARTS

1 cup sugar

1/2 cup water

1/2 cup egg whites, at room
   temperature

1/4 teaspoon salt

1/4 teaspoon cream of tartar

2 teaspoons vanilla extract

Combine sugar and water in a small heavy saucepan and stir to dissolve the sugar. Cook over medium heat until the syrup registers 238°F on a candy thermometer.

While the syrup is cooking, combine the egg whites, salt, and cream of tartar in the bowl of an electric mixer. Using a whip attachment, beat the egg white mixture at high speed until it holds soft peaks. Pour the hot syrup slowly into the egg whites, beating at high speed. (If using an electric mixer that tends to throw some of the syrup around the edge of the bowl, remove the bowl from the mixer and add the syrup while beating with a large spoon. When all of the syrup is incorporated, return the bowl to the mixer stand.)

Add the vanilla and continue to beat at medium speed for 5 minutes or until the meringue is cool. Use immediately, if possible, or refrigerate until needed.

NUTRITIVE VALUES FOR TOTAL RECIPE

---

calories 838 • carbohydrate 200 grams • protein 14 grams • fat trace
sodium 725 milligrams • cholesterol 0 milligrams

Low-sodium diets: Omit salt.

NUTRITIVE VALUES PER QUARTER-CUP SERVING

Number of servings 32

---

calories 26 • carbohydrate 6 grams • protein trace • fat 0 grams
sodium 23 milligrams • cholesterol 0 milligrams

Low-sodium diets: Omit salt.

WHIPPED TOPPING

You should prepare this light and delicate topping the day you want to use it. You can substitute lemon or orange flavorings for the vanilla if you wish.

YIELD: TWO CUPS

¹/₄ **cup ice water**

¹/₂ **cup instant nonfat dry milk**

2 tablespoons lemon juice

¹/₄ **cup powdered or confectioners' sugar**

¹/₂ **teaspoon vanilla extract**

Place water then dry milk in a chilled bowl and whip for 4 minutes using an electric mixer at high speed. Add the lemon juice and continue to whip at high speed for another 4 minutes. Then, using a spoon or rubber spatula, gently stir the powdered sugar and vanilla into the topping. Refrigerate until needed.

NUTRITIVE VALUES FOR TOTAL RECIPE

---

calories 220 • carbohydrate 45 grams • protein 12 grams • fat trace
sodium 187 milligrams • cholesterol 12 milligrams

Low-sodium diets: Recipe may be used as written.

NUTRITIVE VALUES PER QUARTER-CUP SERVING
Number of servings 8

---

calories 28 • carbohydrate 6 grams • protein 2 grams • fat 0 grams
sodium 24 milligrams • cholesterol 1 milligram

Low-sodium diets: Recipe may be used as written.

CHOCOLATE SAUCE

This very versatile sauce is one I like to make when my friends Butch and Jan Franks and their son, John, come over for the evening. They love ice cream and I enjoy giving it to them with this topping and all its variations.

YIELD: TWO CUPS

1 cup water

2 tablespoons instant nonfat dry milk

2 tablespoons cornstarch

$1/2$ cup sugar

$1/4$ cup cocoa

$1/4$ teaspoon salt

$1/2$ cup light corn syrup

2 tablespoons margarine

1 teaspoon vanilla extract

Bring water to a boil in a saucepan. Stir dry milk, cornstarch, sugar, cocoa, and salt together to blend and add to the boiling water. Cook over medium heat, stirring with a wire whip, until smooth. Add corn syrup and margarine and simmer over low heat, stirring frequently, for 2 minutes or until thickened. Remove from heat and add vanilla. Cool to room temperature and refrigerate until needed. Return to room temperature before serving.

VARIATIONS

1. SWEET CHOCOLATE SAUCE: Increase sugar and corn syrup to 1 cup each.

2. LIGHT CHOCOLATE SAUCE: Reduce cocoa to 3 tablespoons and increase dry milk to $1/3$ cup.

3. SEMISWEET CHOCOLATE SAUCE: Increase cocoa to $1/3$ cup and omit cornstarch.

4. CHOCOLATE PEANUT BUTTER SAUCE: Beat $1/2$ cup peanut butter into the sauce after it has cooled.

5. CHOCOLATE NUT SAUCE: Add 1 cup chopped nuts to the sauce just before it is served.

6. CHOCOLATE CHERRY SAUCE: Add 1 cup chopped maraschino cherries to the sauce just before it is served.

7. CHOCOLATE PEPPERMINT SAUCE: Add 1 teaspoon peppermint flavoring along with the vanilla.

8. CHOCOLATE RUM SAUCE: Add 1 teaspoon rum flavoring along with the vanilla.

NUTRITIVE VALUES FOR TOTAL RECIPE

calories 1,239 • carbohydrate 251 grams • protein 9 grams • fat 26 grams
sodium 1,125 milligrams • cholesterol 2 milligrams

Low-sodium diets: Omit salt and
use salt-free margarine. Use low-sodium
peanut butter in the
Chocolate Peanut Butter Sauce.

NUTRITIVE VALUES PER
TWO-TABLESPOON SERVING

Number of servings 16

calories 75 • carbohydrate 16 grams • protein 1 gram • fat 2 grams
sodium 70 milligrams • cholesterol 0 milligrams

Low-sodium diets: Omit salt
and use salt-free margarine. Use low-sodium
peanut butter in the
Chocolate Peanut Butter Sauce.

CUSTARD SAUCE

This sauce complements fresh fruit, fruit gelatin, and gingerbread, among other things. It is good warm, lukewarm, or chilled, depending upon how and when you plan to use it. It is especially good on baked apples — using chilled sauce and warm apples or warm sauce and chilled apples — and it is very good on ginger or other spice cakes.

YIELD: TWO AND A QUARTER CUPS

2 cups water

1/3 cup instant nonfat dry milk

1/3 cup sugar

2 tablespoons cornstarch

1/8 teaspoon salt

2 teaspoons margarine

1/4 cup liquid egg substitute

3 drops yellow food coloring

1 1/2 teaspoons vanilla extract

Combine water, dry milk, sugar, cornstarch, and salt in a small saucepan and stir until smooth. Add the margarine and cook over medium heat, stirring constantly, until thickened and smooth. Remove from the heat. Beat about 1/2 cup sauce into the egg substitute. Return the egg substitute mixture to the saucepan and bring to a simmer, stirring constantly. Remove from the heat, add food coloring and vanilla and mix lightly.

Serve warm, lukewarm, or chilled. Refrigerate sauce if it will not be used within 30 minutes.

VARIATION

RUM CUSTARD SAUCE: Decrease vanilla to 1 teaspoon and add 1 teaspoon rum flavoring.

NUTRITIVE VALUES FOR TOTAL RECIPE

calories 494 • carbohydrate 93 grams • protein 14 grams • fat 10 grams
sodium 274 milligrams • cholesterol 8 milligrams

Low-sodium diets: Omit salt
and use salt-free margarine.

NUTRITIVE VALUES PER QUARTER-CUP SERVING

Number of servings 9

calories 55 • carbohydrate 10 grams • protein 2 grams • fat 1 gram
sodium 30 milligrams • cholesterol 1 milligram

Low-sodium diets: Omit salt
and use salt-free margarine.

LEMON SAUCE

YIELD: TWO CUPS

2 cups cold water

2 tablespoons cornstarch

$1/2$ cup sugar

Grated rind of 1 lemon or 1
tablespoon finely chopped
dried lemon rind

$1/4$ teaspoon salt

2 tablespoons lemon juice

$1 1/2$ tablespoons margarine

Combine water, cornstarch, sugar, and lemon rind in a small saucepan and stir until smooth. Cook over medium heat, stirring constantly, until clear and thickened. Continue to cook over low heat, stirring, for 2 minutes. Remove from heat and add salt, lemon juice, and margarine. Stir until margarine is melted. Serve warm or at room temperature.

VARIATION

ORANGE SAUCE: Substitute orange rind and thawed frozen orange juice concentrate for the lemon rind and juice.

NUTRITIVE VALUES FOR TOTAL RECIPE

calories 604 • carbohydrate 116 grams • protein trace • fat 18 grams
sodium 683 milligrams • cholesterol 0 milligrams

Low-sodium diets: Omit salt
and use salt-free margarine.

NUTRITIVE VALUES PER QUARTER-CUP SERVING

Number of servings 8

calories 76 • carbohydrate 15 grams • protein 0 grams • fat 2 grams
sodium 85 milligrams • cholesterol 0 milligrams

Low-sodium diets: Omit salt
and use salt-free margarine.

COOKIES

COOKIE

PREPARATION

NEARLY EVERYONE LOVES cookies. Those little sources of sheer delight can be used to accompany coffee, tea, or cocoa, or to make an impressive display on beautiful plates or platters for formal occasions.

As is the case with cakes, many of the usual ingredients we have used for years must be eliminated from cholesterol-free cookies because they are high in saturated fat. Fortunately, there is such a wide variety of ingredients left to use that making good cookies shouldn't be a problem for you.

Of course, all of the substitutions used to make cholesterol-free cakes can be used to make cholesterol-free cookies: Egg whites or liquid egg substitute take the place of whole eggs; margarine replaces butter; and oil and buttermilk are used instead of sour cream. We cannot use chocolate, chocolate chips, or coconut, but we can use cocoa, dried fruits, nuts, and liquid flavorings.

Crisp, buttery cookies have a high percentage of sugar and fat to make them crisp, so our cholesterol-free cookies will be softer and not quite as crisp as some traditional cookies. However, there are ways to compensate for reduced fat and sugar, and I have exploited many of them in the following recipes.

Cookies, like cakes, are made using delicately balanced formulas. I have reduced the fat and sugar content as much as I think it can possibly be reduced in the following recipes. Please try the recipe the way it is written the first time. If you feel you can lower the amount of fat and sugar even more, then try it again with less fat or sugar.

If — once you have tried a recipe — you want sweeter cakes or cookies, you can add some sugar substitute to the recipe. The amount of sugar substitute equal to a given amount of sugar is listed on the container. Another important item to look for on the container is whether the product is suitable for baking. I like to use Weight Watcher's dry sugar substitute for baking because it will stand heat and can be measured easily. Equal (aspartame) is a good sugar substitute for beverages and cereal, but in its present form it does not react well to heat. Sweet One sugar substitute will stand heat but it is available only in single-serving packages. There are also some good brown sugar substitutes that are readily available in supermarkets and drugstores.

Generally, all of the basic rules for cake baking outlined in Cake Preparation (page 5) should be followed when making cookies and bars. In addition, the following specific rules apply to cookies and bars:

1. It is a good idea to have cookie sheets and ingredients at room temperature. If cookie dough is placed on hot cookie sheets it will start to cook before it is put in the oven. Cookies should be removed immediately from hot cookie sheets to a wire rack to keep them from overcooking. This rule can be broken only when a recipe indicates that the cookies should be left on the cookie sheet for 2 or 3 minutes to become firm. I use two kinds of cookie sheets: those with a non-stick surface and plain aluminum cookie sheets. Both types can be sprayed with cooking spray or lined with aluminum foil. I use both methods for my own baking and list both methods in most of the recipes. I don't grease cookie sheets because I don't want to add any calories to the cookies, even a very small amount. Also, greased cookie sheets build up a residue that can be difficult to remove.

2. All cookies on a cookie sheet should be of uniform size so that they will bake evenly. I find that dippers are excellent for portioning cookie dough. The cookies will bake more uniformly and will have more accurate nutritive values. Please see page 118 for information regarding different-

size dippers and where they can be purchased. For cookies I strongly recommend using a No. 40 and a No. 60 dipper.

3. If there aren't enough cookies to fill a cookie sheet, use a smaller cookie sheet or space the cookies evenly in the center of the larger cookie sheet.

4. Most cookies can be frozen unless the recipe indicates otherwise. I freeze them in plastic freezer bags and then defrost them at room temperature in the same bags. Sometimes I freeze an assortment of cookies in a bag and sometimes I freeze a bag of just one kind of cookie. I always keep cookies on hand for emergencies such as unexpected company or a call from my church group for a cookie donation.

DROP
COOKIES

ALMOND COOKIES

BUTTERMILK DROP COOKIES

BUTTERMILK DATE DROP COOKIES

BUTTERMILK NUT DROP COOKIES

BUTTERMILK RAISIN DROP COOKIES

CHOCOLATE OATMEAL COOKIES

CHIPLESS COOKIES

CHRISTMAS DROP COOKIES

CITRUS COOKIES

DATE LEMON SUGAR COOKIES

MOM'S OATMEAL COOKIES

DOUBLE PEANUT COOKIES

GERMANTOWN COOKIES

HIGH-FIBER DROP COOKIES

MAPLE PECAN COOKIES

PUMPKIN SPICE COOKIES

DROP SUGAR COOKIES

BLACK WALNUT DROP SUGAR COOKIES

RAISIN DROP SUGAR COOKIES

CANDIED FRUIT DROP SUGAR COOKIES

LEMON DROP SUGAR COOKIES

WHOLE-WHEAT OATMEAL COOKIES

DROP COOKIES ARE the everyday cookies we associate with lunch bags and after-school snacks, not with fancy cookie platters. They are the easiest cookies to make.

The texture of cookies depends upon the proportion of flour to fat and sugar. If a recipe has more flour and less fat and sugar, the cookies will be soft; if a recipe has less flour and more fat and sugar, the cookies will be crisp. I always thought people preferred crisp cookies until I worked as a dietary consultant in a nursing home. One of the patients told me she was tired of crisp cookies and wanted some softer cookies that would be easier to chew. I hadn't thought about that before then, but we changed our cookie policy that day and started making softer cookies that could be chewed more easily.

Baking soda helps cookies spread and baking powder helps them rise. Greasing the pan and adding a higher fat content to the cookie dough also helps cookies spread. Some cookies contain so much fat that they don't need any pan spray or grease on the cookie sheet to help them spread, but this is not true for any of these cookies. In fact, the fat has been reduced enough that I want to reiterate that I prefer non-stick cookie sheets because the cookies can be removed easily, burned dough comes off with little work, and they wash well. I almost always use cooking spray for my cookie sheets and cake pans, although I sometimes line cookie sheets with aluminum foil.

Please review the basic rules in Cake Preparation and Cookie Preparation (pages 5 and 206) before making any of the cookies in this chapter.

ALMOND COOKIES

These cookies are like the cookies served in Chinese restaurants. They are traditionally made with lard and whole eggs, but I have substituted margarine and egg whites or liquid egg substitute so we can have them with our Chinese food.

YIELD: THREE DOZEN COOKIES

1 cup (2 sticks) margarine

1¹/₃ cups sugar

¹/₄ cup egg whites or liquid egg
    substitute

2 teaspoons almond extract

4 cups all-purpose flour

2 teaspoons baking powder

1 teaspoon baking soda

¹/₂ teaspoon salt

¹/₂ cup water

36 almonds

Preheat oven to 350°F. Spray cookie sheets with cooking spray or line with aluminum foil. Set aside.

Using an electric mixer at medium speed, cream margarine and sugar together until light and fluffy. Add egg whites or liquid egg substitute and almond extract and mix at medium speed until creamy, scraping down the bowl before and after the addition.

Stir flour, baking powder, baking soda, and salt together to blend and add to the egg mixture, along with the water. Mix at medium speed to blend.

Drop the dough onto the prepared cookie sheets by 1¹/₂ tablespoonsful (or use a level No. 40 dipper). Gently press down on each cookie with the back of a tablespoon dipped in cold water. Then press an almond in the center of each cookie. Bake for 12 to 15 minutes or until very lightly browned and firm. Cool on wire racks.

NUTRITIVE VALUES PER SERVING

Number of servings 36

---

calories 132 • carbohydrate 18 grams • protein 2 grams • fat 6 grams
sodium 133 milligrams • cholesterol 0 milligrams

Low-sodium diets: Omit salt.
Use salt-free margarine and low-sodium baking powder.

BUTTERMILK DROP COOKIES

YIELD: FOUR DOZEN COOKIES

2 cups sugar

1 cup (2 sticks) margarine

1/2 cup egg whites or liquid egg
substitute, at room
temperature

2 teaspoons vanilla extract

4 cups all-purpose flour

2 teaspoons baking soda

1/4 cup dry buttermilk

1/2 teaspoon salt

1/4 cup water, at room
temperature

Preheat oven to 375°F. Spray cookie sheets with cooking spray or line
with aluminum foil. Set aside.

Using an electric mixer at medium speed, cream sugar and margarine
together until light and fluffy. Add egg whites or liquid egg substitute and
vanilla and mix at medium speed until creamy, scraping down the bowl
before and after the addition.

Stir flour, baking soda, dry buttermilk, and salt together to blend and add
to the creamy mixture, along with the water. Mix at medium speed until
blended.

Drop the dough onto the prepared cookie sheets by 1½ tablespoonsful (or use a level No. 40 dipper). Gently press down on each cookie with the back of a tablespoon dipped in cold water. Bake for 18 minutes or until lightly browned. Cool on wire racks.

VARIATIONS

1. BUTTERMILK DATE DROP COOKIES: Stir 1 cup finely chopped dates into the flour mixture.

2. BUTTERMILK NUT DROP COOKIES: Stir 1 cup finely chopped nuts into the flour mixture.

3. BUTTERMILK RAISIN DROP COOKIES: Stir 1 cup chopped raisins into the flour mixture.

NUTRITIVE VALUES PER SERVING

Number of servings 48

calories 107 • carbohydrate 17 grams • protein 2 grams • fat 4 grams
sodium 86 milligrams • cholesterol 0 milligrams

Low-sodium diets: Use salt-free margarine.

CHOCOLATE OATMEAL COOKIES

YIELD: THREE DOZEN COOKIES

1 cup sugar

1 cup brown sugar

³/₄ cup (1¹/₂ sticks) margarine

2 large egg whites or ¹/₄ cup
  liquid egg substitute

1 teaspoon vanilla extract

2 cups all-purpose flour

¹/₄ cup cocoa

¹/₂ teaspoon baking powder

1 teaspoon baking soda

¹/₂ teaspoon salt

¹/₃ cup water, at room
  temperature

2 cups rolled oats

Preheat oven to 375°F. Spray cookie sheets with cooking spray or line with aluminum foil. Set aside.

Using an electric mixer at medium speed, cream sugars and margarine together until light and fluffy. Add egg whites or liquid egg substitute and vanilla and mix at medium speed until creamy, scraping down the bowl before and after the addition.

Stir flour, cocoa, baking powder, baking soda, and salt together and add to the creamed mixture, along with the water. Mix only until the flour is moistened. Then add the oatmeal and mix until the oatmeal is also absorbed.

Drop the dough onto the prepared cookie sheets by 1¹/₂ tablespoonsful (or use a level No. 40 dipper). Bake for 10 to 12 minutes or until almost firm. Cool on wire racks.

NUTRITIVE VALUES PER SERVING

Number of servings 36

---

calories 105 • carbohydrate 17 grams • protein 1 gram • fat 4 grams
sodium 107 milligrams • cholesterol 0 milligrams

Low-sodium diets: Omit salt.
Use salt-free margarine and low-sodium baking powder.

CHIPLESS COOKIES

I call these chipless cookies because they taste like chocolate chip cookies without the chocolate chips.

YIELD: THREE DOZEN COOKIES

³/₄ cup (1¹/₂ sticks) margarine

³/₄ cup sugar

³/₄ cup brown sugar

¹/₃ cup liquid egg substitute

1 teaspoon vanilla extract

2¹/₂ cups all-purpose flour

1 teaspoon baking soda

1 teaspoon salt

¹/₄ cup chopped pecans

¹/₄ cup raisins

Preheat oven to 375°F. Spray cookie sheets with cooking spray or line with aluminum foil. Set aside.

Using an electric mixer at medium speed, cream margarine and sugars together until light and fluffy. Add liquid egg substitute and vanilla and mix at medium speed for 30 seconds, scraping down the bowl before and after the addition.

Stir flour, baking soda, salt, pecans, and raisins together and add to the creamy mixture. Mix at medium speed to blend.

Drop the dough onto the prepared cookie sheets by 1½ tablespoonful (or use a level No. 40 dipper). Bake for 10 minutes or until lightly browned. Cool on wire racks.

NUTRITIVE VALUES PER SERVING

Number of servings 36

---

calories 104 • carbohydrate 15 grams • protein 1 gram • fat 5 grams
sodium 131 milligrams • cholesterol 0 milligrams

Low-sodium diets: Omit salt
and use salt-free margarine.

CHRISTMAS DROP COOKIES

I call these Christmas drop cookies because my friend Jan Franks of Oelwein, Iowa, says that one taste of them puts her in a holiday mood.

YIELD: NEARLY THREE DOZEN COOKIES

1½ cups all-purpose flour

½ cup sugar

½ cup brown sugar

1 teaspoon baking soda

1 cup chopped candied fruit

⅔ cup vegetable oil

½ cup egg whites or liquid egg substitute

1 teaspoon vanilla extract

¼ cup water

Preheat oven to 375°F. Spray cookie sheets with cooking spray or line with aluminum foil. Set aside.

Place flour, sugars, baking soda, and candied fruit in the bowl of an electric mixer and mix at low speed to blend well. Beat oil, egg whites or liquid egg substitute, vanilla, and water together with a fork to blend well and add to the flour mixture. Mix at medium speed until creamy.

Drop the dough onto the prepared cookie sheets by 1½ tablespoonsful (or use a level No. 40 dipper). Bake for 10 to 12 minutes or until lightly browned. Cool on wire racks.

NUTRITIVE VALUES PER SERVING

Number of servings 33

calories 122 • carbohydrate 19 grams • protein 1 gram • fat 4 grams
sodium 33 milligrams • cholesterol 0 milligrams

Low-sodium diets: May be used as written.

CITRUS COOKIES

YIELD: TWO DOZEN COOKIES

½ cup (1 stick) margarine

¾ cup sugar, plus additional as needed

2 large egg whites

1 teaspoon lemon extract

2½ cups all-purpose flour

1 tablespoon dry buttermilk

½ teaspoon baking powder

½ teaspoon baking soda

¼ teaspoon salt

1 tablespoon grated fresh or finely chopped dried orange rind

2 tablespoons water

Preheat oven to 375°F. Spray cookie sheets with cooking spray or line with aluminum foil. Set aside.

Using an electric mixer at medium speed, cream margarine and $^3/_4$ cup sugar together until light and fluffy. Add egg whites and lemon extract and mix at medium speed until creamy, scraping down the bowl before and after the addition.

Stir flour, dry buttermilk, baking powder, baking soda, salt, and orange rind together to blend well and add, along with the water, to the creamy mixture. Mix at medium speed until smooth.

Drop the dough onto the prepared cookie sheets by $1^1/_2$ tablespoonsful (or use a level No. 40 dipper). Gently press down on each cookie with the back of a tablespoon dipped in water and then sugar. Bake for 15 minutes or until firm and browned on the bottom. Cool on wire racks.

NUTRITIVE VALUES PER SERVING

Number of servings 24

---

calories 107 • carbohydrate 16 grams • protein 2 grams • fat 4 grams
sodium 96 milligrams • cholesterol 0 milligrams

Low-sodium diets: Omit salt.
Use salt-free margarine and low-sodium baking powder.

DATE LEMON SUGAR COOKIES

This recipe comes from my friend Jan Franks of Oelwein, Iowa. It is a soft, flavorful sugar cookie, which is good for children or anyone who has difficulty chewing a crisp cookie.

YIELD: TWO DOZEN COOKIES

½ cup (1 stick) margarine

½ cup sugar

2 teaspoons lemon extract

¼ cup egg whites or liquid egg substitute

1 tablespoon lemon juice

2 tablespoons grated fresh or finely chopped dried lemon rind

2¼ cups all-purpose flour

½ teaspoon baking soda

½ cup chopped dates

½ cup water, at room temperature

Preheat oven to 350°F. Spray cookie sheets with cooking spray or line with aluminum foil. Set aside.

Using an electric mixer at medium speed, cream margarine, sugar, and lemon extract together until light and fluffy. Add egg whites or liquid egg substitute, lemon juice, and rind and mix at medium speed for 30 seconds, scraping down the bowl before and after the addition.

Stir flour, baking soda, and dates together to blend and add, along with the water, to the egg mixture. Mix at medium speed to blend.

Drop the dough onto the prepared cookie sheets by 1½ tablespoonsful (or use a level No. 40 dipper). Using the back of a tablespoon dipped in cold water, gently press each cookie down to about ⅓ inch thick. Bake for 10 to 12 minutes or until lightly browned and firm. Cool on wire racks.

NUTRITIVE VALUES PER SERVING

Number of servings 24

---

calories 104 • carbohydrate 16 grams • protein 2 grams • fat 4 grams
• sodium 66 milligrams • cholesterol 0 milligrams

Low-sodium diets: Use salt-free margarine.

MOM'S OATMEAL COOKIES

YIELD: TWO DOZEN COOKIES

½ cup (1 stick) margarine

½ cup sugar

½ cup brown sugar

¼ cup egg whites or liquid egg substitute

¼ cup water, at room temperature

1 teaspoon vanilla extract

½ teaspoon black walnut flavoring

1½ cups all-purpose flour

1 teaspoon baking powder

1 teaspoon baking soda

¼ teaspoon salt

2 cups rolled oats

⅓ cup chopped black or English walnuts

Preheat oven to 350°F. Spray cookie sheets with cooking spray or line with aluminum foil. Set aside.

Using an electric mixer at medium speed, cream margarine and sugars together until light and fluffy. Add egg whites or liquid egg substitute, water, and flavorings and mix at medium speed for 30 seconds, scraping down the bowl before and after the addition.

Stir flour, baking powder, baking soda, salt, oatmeal, and nuts together to blend and add to the egg mixture. Mix at medium speed to blend.

Drop the dough onto the prepared cookie sheets by 1½ tablespoonsful (or use a level No. 40 dipper). Using the back of a tablespoon dipped in cold water, gently press each cookie down to about ½ inch thick. Bake for 12 to 14 minutes or until lightly browned. Cool on wire racks.

NUTRITIVE VALUES PER SERVING

Number of servings 24

---

calories 133 • carbohydrate 19 grams • protein 2 grams • fat 5 grams
sodium 121 milligrams • cholesterol 0 milligrams

Low-sodium diets: Omit salt.
Use salt-free margarine and low-sodium baking powder.

DOUBLE PEANUT COOKIES

YIELD: TWO AND A HALF DOZEN COOKIES

¼ cup (½ stick) margarine

1 cup sugar

½ cup smooth peanut butter

1 teaspoon vanilla extract

½ cup water, at room
   temperature

2 cups all-purpose flour

1 teaspoon baking soda

½ teaspoon salt

1 cup chopped, roasted, salted
   peanuts

Preheat oven to 350°F. Spray cookie sheets with cooking spray or line with aluminum foil. Set aside.

Using an electric mixer at medium speed, cream margarine, sugar, and peanut butter together until light and fluffy. Add vanilla and water and mix at medium speed for 30 seconds, scraping down the bowl before and after the addition.

Stir flour, baking soda, and salt together to blend and add to the peanut butter mixture, along with the peanuts. Mix at medium speed to blend well.

Drop the dough onto the prepared cookie sheets by 1½ tablespoonsful (or use a level No. 40 dipper). Gently press each cookie down with the back of a tablespoon dipped in cold water. Bake for 12 to 14 minutes or until lightly browned. Cool on the cookie sheets for 2 to 3 minutes. Then remove to wire racks to cool to room temperature.

NUTRITIVE VALUES PER SERVING

Number of servings 30

---

calories 120 • carbohydrate 14 grams • protein 3 grams • fat 6 grams
sodium 122 milligrams • cholesterol 0 milligrams

Low-sodium diets: Omit salt.
Use salt-free margarine and unsalted peanuts.

GERMANTOWN COOKIES

YIELD: TWO AND A HALF DOZEN COOKIES

³/₄ cup (1½ sticks) margarine

³/₄ cup sugar

³/₄ cup brown sugar

¹/₃ cup egg whites or liquid egg substitute

1 teaspoon vanilla extract

2¼ cups all-purpose flour

³/₄ teaspoon baking powder

³/₄ teaspoon baking soda

1 cup rolled oats

Preheat oven to 350°F. Spray cookie sheets with cooking spray or line with aluminum foil. Set aside.

Using an electric mixer at medium speed, cream margarine and sugars together until light and fluffy. Add egg whites or liquid egg substitute and vanilla and mix at medium speed until creamy, scraping down the bowl before and after the addition.

Stir flour, baking powder, baking soda, and oatmeal together to blend and add to the creamy mixture. Mix at medium speed until well blended.

Drop the dough onto the prepared cookie sheets by 1½ tablespoonsful (or use a level No. 40 dipper). Bake for 15 minutes or until almost firm. Cool on wire racks.

NUTRITIVE VALUES PER SERVING

Number of servings 30

---

calories 130 • carbohydrate 19 grams • protein 2 grams • fat 5 grams
sodium 91 milligrams • cholesterol 0 milligrams

Low-sodium diets: Use salt-free margarine
and low-sodium baking powder.

HIGH-FIBER
DROP COOKIES

YIELD: FOUR DOZEN COOKIES

1 cup oat bran cereal

1 cup rolled oats

1 cup Fiber One cereal

1 cup Kellogg's Bran Flakes
cereal

1 cup raisins

1 cup chopped English walnuts

³/₄ cup sugar

³/₄ cup brown sugar

1 cup (2 sticks) margarine

2 teaspoons vanilla extract

¹/₄ cup egg whites or liquid egg
substitute

2 cups all-purpose flour

1 teaspoon baking powder

1 teaspoon baking soda

¹/₂ teaspoon salt

¹/₂ cup water, at room
temperature

Preheat oven to 375°F. Spray cookie sheets with cooking spray or line with aluminum foil. Set aside.

Place oat bran cereal, oatmeal, Fiber One, Bran Flakes, raisins, and nuts in a large bowl and mix lightly. Set aside.

Using an electric mixer at medium speed, cream sugars and margarine together until light and fluffy. Add vanilla and egg whites or liquid egg substitute to the creamed mixture and mix at medium speed until creamy, scraping down the bowl before and after the addition.

Stir flour, baking powder, baking soda, and salt together to blend and add to the creamy mixture, along with the water. Mix only until the flour is moistened. Add the cereal mixture and mix at medium speed until combined.

Drop the batter onto the prepared cookie sheets by 1¹/₂ tablespoonsful (or use a level No. 40 dipper). Bake for 12 to 14 minutes or until lightly browned. Cool on wire racks.

NUTRITIVE VALUES PER SERVING

Number of servings 48

---

calories 124 • carbohydrate 18 grams • protein 2 grams • fat 6 grams
sodium 126 milligrams • cholesterol 0 milligrams

Low-sodium diets: Omit salt.
Use salt-free margarine and low-sodium baking powder.

MAPLE PECAN COOKIES

There are no pecan trees where they make maple syrup and no maple trees for syrup where they grow pecans, but the two certainly complement each other.

YIELD: TWO AND A HALF DOZEN COOKIES

4 tablespoons (½ stick)
  margarine

½ cup brown sugar

½ cup maple syrup

¼ cup egg whites or liquid egg
  substitute

1 teaspoon maple flavoring

2 cups all-purpose flour

1 tablespoon dry buttermilk

1 teaspoon baking soda

¼ teaspoon salt

½ cup chopped pecans

Preheat oven to 350°F. Spray cookie sheets with cooking spray or line with aluminum foil. Set aside.

Using an electric mixer at medium speed, beat margarine, brown sugar, and maple syrup together until creamy. Add egg whites or liquid egg substitute and flavoring and mix at medium speed for 30 seconds, scraping down the bowl before and after the addition.

Stir flour, dry buttermilk, baking soda, salt, and pecans together to blend and add to the egg mixture. Mix at medium speed to blend.

Drop the batter onto the prepared cookie sheets by the tablespoonful (or use a level No. 60 dipper). Bake for 10 to 12 minutes or until lightly browned. Cool on wire racks.

NUTRITIVE VALUES PER SERVING

Number of servings 30

---

calories 87 • carbohydrate 14 grams • protein 1 gram • fat 3 grams
sodium 70 milligrams • cholesterol 0 milligrams

Low-sodium diets: Omit salt
and use salt-free margarine.

PUMPKIN SPICE COOKIES

I like to serve these soft, spicy cookies with a pitcher of apple cider in the fall.

YIELD: TWO AND A HALF DOZEN COOKIES

½ cup (1 stick) margarine

1 cup brown sugar

½ cup egg whites or liquid egg substitute

1 teaspoon maple flavoring

¾ cup canned pumpkin puree

1½ cups all-purpose flour

1 teaspoon baking powder

½ teaspoon baking soda

1 teaspoon pumpkin pie spice

1 teaspoon cinnamon

½ cup raisins

Preheat oven to 350°F. Spray cookie sheets with cooking spray or line with aluminum foil. Set aside.

Using an electric mixer at medium speed, cream margarine and brown sugar until light and fluffy. Add egg whites or liquid egg substitute, maple flavoring, and pumpkin and mix at medium speed until creamy, scraping the bowl before and after the addition.

Stir flour, baking powder, baking soda, pumpkin pie spice, cinnamon, and raisins together and add to the creamy mixture. Mix to blend.

Drop the dough onto the prepared cookie sheets by 1½ tablespoonsful (or use a level No. 40 dipper). Bake for 15 minutes or until firm. Cool on wire racks.

NUTRITIVE VALUES PER SERVING

Number of servings 30

---

calories 88 • carbohydrate 14 grams • protein 1 gram • fat 3 grams
sodium 70 milligrams • cholesterol 0 milligrams

Low-sodium diets: Use salt-free margarine
and low-sodium baking powder.

DROP SUGAR COOKIES

These crisp sugar cookies can be tinted with food coloring for special occasions. They can also be topped with almond, pecan, or walnut halves.

YIELD: SIX DOZEN COOKIES

1 cup sugar

1 cup powdered or
confectioners' sugar

1 cup (2 sticks) margarine

³/₄ cup vegetable oil

¹/₂ cup egg whites or liquid egg
substitute, at room
temperature

1 teaspoon vanilla extract

4¹/₂ cups all-purpose flour

1 teaspoon baking soda

1 teaspoon cream of tartar

Preheat oven to 375°F. Spray cookie sheets with cooking spray or line with aluminum foil. Set aside.

Place sugars, margarine, and oil in the bowl of an electric mixer and mix at medium speed until creamy. Add egg whites or liquid egg substitute and vanilla and mix at medium speed until creamy, scraping down the bowl before and after the addition.

Stir flour, baking soda, and cream of tartar together to blend and add to the creamy mixture and mix at medium speed until smooth.

Drop the dough onto the prepared cookie sheets by the tablespoonful (or use a level No. 60 dipper). Gently press each cookie down lightly with the back of a tablespoon dipped in cold water. Bake for 12 to 15 minutes or until lightly browned around the edges. Cool on wire racks.

VARIATIONS

1. BLACK WALNUT DROP SUGAR COOKIES: Add 1 teaspoon black walnut flavoring with the vanilla and 3/4 cup chopped black walnuts with the flour mixture.

2. RAISIN DROP SUGAR COOKIES: Add 3/4 cup chopped raisins with the flour mixture.

3. CANDIED FRUIT DROP SUGAR COOKIES: Add 3/4 cup chopped candied fruit with the flour mixture.

4. LEMON DROP SUGAR COOKIES: Omit vanilla and add 2 teaspoons lemon extract and 1 tablespoon finely chopped fresh or dried lemon peel.

NUTRITIVE VALUES PER SERVING

Number of servings 72

---

calories 88 • carbohydrate 10 grams • protein 1 gram • fat 5 grams
sodium 44 milligrams • cholesterol 0 milligrams

Low-sodium diets: Use salt-free margarine.

WHOLE-WHEAT OATMEAL COOKIES

YIELD: FOUR DOZEN COOKIES

3/4 **cup sugar**

3/4 **cup brown sugar**

3/4 **cup (1 1/2 sticks) margarine**

1/2 **cup egg whites or liquid egg substitute**

2 **teaspoons vanilla extract**

1 1/2 **cups whole-wheat flour**

1 **teaspoon cinnamon**

1 **teaspoon baking soda**

2 **cups rolled oats**

1/2 **cup chopped pecans**

1/2 **cup raisins**

Preheat oven to 375°F. Spray cookie sheets with cooking spray or line with aluminum foil. Set aside.

Using an electric mixer at medium speed, cream sugars and margarine together until light and fluffy. Add egg whites or liquid egg substitute and vanilla and mix at medium speed until creamy, scraping down the bowl before and after the addition.

Stir flour, cinnamon, and baking soda together to blend and add to the creamy mixture. Beat at medium speed only until the flour is moistened. Add oatmeal, pecans, and raisins and mix at medium speed to blend.

Drop the dough onto the prepared cookie sheets by the tablespoonful (or use a level No. 60 dipper). (For flat cookies, press the dough down lightly with the back of a tablespoon dipped in cold water.) Bake for 10 to 12 minutes or until almost firm. Cool on the cookie sheets for 2 to 3 minutes. Then remove to wire racks to cool to room temperature.

NUTRITIVE VALUES PER SERVING

Number of servings 48

---

calories 90 • carbohydrate 13 grams • protein 1 gram • fat 4 grams
sodium 56 milligrams • cholesterol 0 milligrams

Low-sodium diets: Use salt-free margarine.

EUROPEAN-STYLE
COOKIES

BISCOTTI

HONEY LEBKUCHEN

MOLASSES LEBKUCHEN

PEPPERNUT COOKIES

CINNAMON RUM COOKIES

SCOTTISH SHORTBREAD

WHOLE-WHEAT SHORTBREAD

SWEDISH ALMOND CRESCENTS

BLACK WALNUT CRESCENTS

VIENNESE CRESCENTS

―――――

WHEN WE LIVED in Chicago I loved going to the many neighborhood bakeries where we could buy a variety of foods. We bought biscotti and almond macaroons in Italian bakeries, and luscious sweet cakes and cookies in Greek bakeries.

Many of those cakes and cookies can be adapted to a low-cholesterol, low-fat, low-sugar diet. I hope the recipes in this chapter will inspire you to get out your own ancestral recipes and try to adapt them to your present diet. Keep in mind that you must substitute egg whites or liquid egg substitute for eggs and reduce fat and sugar but keep the flavorings, seeds, and methods used in preparing your grandmother's cakes and cookies. Please review the basic rules in Cake Preparation and Cookie Preparation (pages 5 and 206) before making any of the cookies in this chapter.

BISCOTTI

These firm, crisp Italian cookies are generally served with wine or coffee. This recipe came from my husband's cousin, Mary Cavaiani Lancour, of Iron Mountain, Michigan.

YIELD: NEARLY THREE AND A HALF DOZEN COOKIES

1 cup sugar

1/2 cup vegetable oil

1 cup egg whites or liquid egg substitute

1 teaspoon anise flavoring

4 1/2 cups all-purpose flour

1 tablespoon baking powder

2 tablespoons skim milk

Preheat oven to 375°F. Spray a cookie sheet with cooking spray or line with aluminum foil. Set aside.

Using an electric mixer at medium speed, beat sugar, oil, egg whites or liquid egg substitute, and anise flavoring together to blend well. Stir flour and baking powder together and add to the creamy mixture. Mix at medium speed to blend.

Turn the dough out onto a floured working surface and knead briefly. Divide the dough into two equal portions and form each portion into a roll 15 inches long. Place rolls on the prepared cookie sheet, brush with milk, and bake for 25 to 30 minutes or until firm and lightly browned. Cool 5 minutes on a wire rack. Then slice each roll into 20 diagonal slices, each about 3/4 inch thick.

Place the slices on their sides on ungreased cookie sheets and bake for 5 minutes, turn, and bake for another 5 minutes. Cool on wire racks.

NOTE: Biscotti may be stored in an airtight container at room temperature or frozen indefinitely. They are generally made two or three days before they are needed, then allowed to stand to develop their flavor.

NUTRITIVE VALUES PER SERVING

Number of servings 40

---

calories 99 • carbohydrate 16 grams • protein 2 grams • fat 3 grams
sodium 36 milligrams • cholesterol 0 milligrams

Low-sodium diets: Use low-sodium baking powder.

HONEY LEBKUCHEN

This is based on a very old German recipe. The original recipe calls for mixing the dough and letting it rest about 2 months before baking the cookies. The resulting fat-free cookies are very hard and need to mellow in the cookie jar at least another month to soften. I developed this simplified recipe with my friend Eva Burrack of Strawberry Point, Iowa. Now the cookies can be baked soon after they are mixed but they still need to rest about a month before they are soft enough to eat.

YIELD: THREE DOZEN COOKIES

2¼ cups all-purpose flour

¼ cup sugar

½ cup chopped candied fruit

½ cup chopped English walnuts

1 teaspoon baking soda

¼ teaspoon cinnamon

¼ teaspoon ground cloves

¼ teaspoon nutmeg

¼ cup egg whites or liquid egg substitute

1 teaspoon lemon juice

⅔ cup honey

Place flour, sugar, fruit, nuts, baking soda, and spices in the bowl of an electric mixer and mix at low speed for 30 seconds to blend. Add egg whites or liquid egg substitute and lemon juice and mix at low speed for another 30 seconds. Heat the honey to boiling and pour over the flour mixture. Mix at medium speed to form a stiff dough.

Turn the dough out onto a piece of aluminum foil that has been sprinkled with flour and form the dough into a 9 by 2-inch oblong. Wrap the aluminum foil around the rectangle of dough and refrigerate or freeze until firm.

Return the dough to the working surface, remove the foil, and cut crosswise into 36 1/4-inch slices. Place the slices on cookie sheets that have been sprayed with cooking spray or lined with aluminum foil. Bake in a preheated 375°F oven for 10 to 12 minutes or until lightly browned on the bottoms. Cool to room temperature. Then place the cookies in an airtight container and let stand for 3 to 4 weeks or until softened.

NOTE: The warm dough may also be rolled out 1/4 inch thick on a floured board and cut out with cookie cutters before baking.

NUTRITIVE VALUES PER SERVING

Number of servings 36

---

calories 75 • carbohydrate 16 grams • protein 1 gram • fat 1 gram
sodium 26 milligrams • cholesterol 0 milligrams

Low-sodium diets: May be used as written.

MOLASSES LEBKUCHEN

This is another German cookie recipe that Eva Burrack and I simplified during our years at the Lutheran Nursing Home in Strawberry Point, Iowa. At the time, Eva was the food service supervisor and I was the dietary consultant.

YIELD: FOUR DOZEN COOKIES

3¹/₄ cups all-purpose flour

1 teaspoon baking soda

1 teaspoon cinnamon

¹/₄ teaspoon ground cloves

¹/₄ teaspoon allspice

¹/₂ cup chopped candied fruit

¹/₂ cup chopped candied citron

¹/₂ cup chopped nuts

1¹/₂ cups molasses, heated to boiling

¹/₃ cup whiskey

Place 3 cups flour, baking soda, spices, candied fruit, and nuts in the bowl of an electric mixer and mix at medium speed to blend. Add molasses and whiskey and mix at medium speed to blend. Sprinkle a large piece of aluminum foil with the remaining ¹/₄ cup flour. Turn the dough out onto the foil and knead several times, incorporating as much of the flour as necessary to make a smooth dough. Divide the dough into two equal portions and shape each portion into a roll 6 inches long and about 1¹/₂ inches thick. Wrap each roll in aluminum foil and refrigerate or freeze until firm. Cut each roll into 24 slices, each ¹/₄ inch thick.

Place the slices on cookie sheets that have been sprayed with cooking spray or lined with aluminum foil. Bake in a preheated 375°F oven for 10 to 12 minutes or until firm. Cool on wire racks. Then place the cookies in an airtight container and let stand for 3 to 4 weeks or until softened.

NOTE: The warm dough may also be rolled out ¹/₄ inch thick on a lightly floured working surface and cut out with cookie cutters.

NUTRITIVE VALUES PER SERVING

Number of servings 48

---

calories 76 • carbohydrate 16 grams • protein 1 gram • fat 1 gram
sodium 27 milligrams • cholesterol 0 milligrams

Low-sodium diets: May be used as written.

PEPPERNUT COOKIES

These crisp Austrian cookies will soften if stored in an airtight container at room temperature.

YIELD: THREE DOZEN COOKIES

1/2 cup (1 stick) margarine

1 cup sugar

1/2 cup egg whites or liquid egg substitute

1 teaspoon rum flavoring

3 cups all-purpose flour

1/2 teaspoon ground cloves

1/4 teaspoon coarsely ground black pepper

1 teaspoon cinnamon

1 teaspoon baking powder

Preheat oven to 375°F. Spray cookie sheets with cooking spray or line with aluminum foil. Set aside.

Using an electric mixer at medium speed, cream margarine and sugar together until light and fluffy. Add egg whites or liquid egg substitute and rum flavoring and mix at medium speed for 1 minute, scraping down the bowl before and after the addition.

Stir flour, spices, and baking powder together to blend. Add the flour mixture to the egg mixture and mix at medium speed to blend.

Turn the dough out onto a floured working surface and roll out about $^1/_3$ inch thick. Cut with a 2$^1/_2$-inch round cutter and place on the prepared cookie sheets. Bake for 15 minutes or until firm and lightly browned on the bottoms. Cool on wire racks.

VARIATION

CINNAMON RUM COOKIES: Omit cloves and pepper. Increase rum flavoring and cinnamon to 2 teaspoons each.

NUTRITIVE VALUES PER SERVING

Number of servings 36

---

calories 84 • carbohydrate 14 grams • protein 2 grams • fat 3 grams
sodium 37 milligrams • cholesterol 0 milligrams

Low-sodium diets: Use salt-free margarine
and low-sodium baking powder.

SCOTTISH SHORTBREAD

One Christmas I made these in 3 by 5-inch rectangles and wrote the names of each of our guests on them in frosting. Everyone loved these edible place cards, especially the children.

YIELD: THREE AND A HALF DOZEN COOKIES

1½ cups (3 sticks) margarine

1 cup sugar

1 teaspoon vanilla or almond
   extract (optional)

3 cups all-purpose flour

Preheat oven to 350°F. Spray cookie sheets with cooking spray or line with aluminum foil. Set aside.

Using an electric mixer at medium speed, cream margarine, sugar, and vanilla or almond extract together until light and fluffy. Scrape down the bowl, add flour, and mix at medium speed to form a stiff dough.

Turn the dough out onto a lightly floured board, knead lightly, and roll out ¼ inch thick. Cut into 2¼-inch squares and place on the prepared cookie sheets. Bake for 18 to 20 minutes or until lightly browned on the bottoms. Cool on wire racks.

VARIATION

WHOLE-WHEAT SHORTBREAD: Substitute 1 cup brown sugar for the sugar. Use 1½ cups all-purpose flour and 1½ cups whole-wheat flour instead of 3 cups all-purpose flour.

NUTRITIVE VALUES PER SERVING

Number of servings 42

---

calories 109 • carbohydrate 12 grams • protein 1 gram • fat 7 grams
sodium 80 milligrams • cholesterol 0 milligrams

Low-sodium diets: Use salt-free margarine.

SWEDISH ALMOND CRESCENTS

YIELD: TWO DOZEN COOKIES

$\frac{1}{2}$ **cup (1 stick) margarine**

$\frac{1}{3}$ **cup sugar**

$\frac{1}{2}$ **teaspoon almond extract**

$1\frac{2}{3}$ **cups all-purpose flour**

$\frac{2}{3}$ **cup ground or very finely chopped almonds**

$\frac{1}{4}$ **cup water**

$\frac{1}{3}$ **cup powdered or confectioners' sugar**

Preheat oven to 375°F. Spray cookie sheets with cooking spray or line with aluminum foil. Set aside.

Using an electric mixer at medium speed, cream margarine, sugar, and almond extract together until light and fluffy. Add flour, nuts, and water to the creamed mixture and mix at medium speed to blend.

Turn the dough out onto a lightly floured board, knead lightly, and divide into 24 portions of 1 tablespoon (a level No. 60 dipper) each. Shape each portion into a roll about 4 inches long with tapered ends. Form the rolls into crescents and place them on the prepared cookie sheets. Bake for 8 to 10 minutes or until lightly browned on the bottoms. Dredge the warm crescents in powdered sugar and place on wire racks to cool to room temperature. Store in an airtight container or freeze until needed.

VARIATION

BLACK WALNUT CRESCENTS: Omit almond extract and almonds. Add ½ teaspoon black walnut flavoring and ⅔ cup finely chopped black walnuts.

NUTRITIVE VALUES PER SERVING

Number of servings 24

---

calories 103 • carbohydrate 12 grams • protein 2 grams • fat 6 grams
sodium 45 milligrams • cholesterol 0 milligrams

Low-sodium diets: Use salt-free margarine.

VIENNESE CRESCENTS

YIELD: THREE DOZEN CRESCENTS

1¾ cups all-purpose flour

½ cup plus 2 tablespoons powdered or confectioners' sugar

¼ teaspoon salt

½ cup (1 stick) margarine, chilled

½ cup finely chopped hazelnuts

1 teaspoon vanilla extract

¼ cup cold water

Place flour, 2 tablespoons powdered sugar, salt, and margarine in the bowl of an electric mixer and mix at medium speed to form a coarse crumb. Add hazelnuts, vanilla, and water and mix at medium speed until the dough pulls together.

Turn the dough out onto a lightly floured working surface and knead a few times to form a smooth ball. Cover and refrigerate from 2 hours to overnight. Return the dough to room temperature.

Divide the dough into 36 equal portions of 1 tablespoon each (a level No. 60 dipper). Shape each portion into a roll about 4 inches long with tapered ends. Form the rolls into crescents and place them on cookie sheets that have been sprayed with cooking spray or lined with aluminum foil. Bake in a preheated 350°F oven for 12 to 15 minutes or until lightly browned on the bottoms. Dredge the warm crescents in the remaining $1/2$ cup powdered sugar and place on wire racks to cool to room temperature. Store crescents in an airtight container or freeze until needed.

NOTE: Other kinds of chopped nuts may be used instead of the hazelnuts with very little change in the nutritive values.

NUTRITIVE VALUES PER SERVING

Number of servings 36

---

calories 61 • carbohydrate 7 grams • protein 1 gram • fat 3 grams
sodium 45 milligrams • cholesterol 0 milligrams

Low-sodium diets: Omit salt
and use salt-free margarine.

FORMED
COOKIES

FRAN'S BLACK WALNUT COOKIES

FRAN'S ALMOND COOKIES

ROLLED BUTTERMILK COOKIES

BUTTERSCOTCH CIRCLES

CHERRY KISSES

CHOCOLATE CHERRY ROLLS

CHOCOLATE PEPPERMINT ROLLS

CHOCOLATE LEMON ROLLS

CHOCOLATE ALMOND ROLLS

CHOCOLATE CRACKLE COOKIES

CHOCOLATE CRISPS

CHOCOLATE PEPPERMINT CRISPS

CHOCOLATE WALNUT CRISPS

CHOCOLATE RAISIN CRISPS

DATE PINWHEEL COOKIES

MARGARINE COOKIES

MOLASSES COOKIES

RIBBON COOKIES

SPOON RIVER COOKIES

FORMED COOKIES ARE a little more work than drop cookies but they are so pretty. I enjoy making them and love the way they add color and variety to a cookie platter. I am particularly fond of Chocolate Cherry Rolls (page 253), Date Pinwheel Cookies (page 258), and shaped Margarine Cookies (page 260).

I have been collecting cookie recipes and fancy cookie cutters since before I was married, so I was happy to find that there are lots of beautiful cookies I can make while sticking to a low-cholesterol, low-fat, low-sugar diet.

Some formed cookies need to be refrigerated or frozen until they are firm. This step is important because the gluten in the flour gets a chance to develop, giving the dough more body and making it much easier to handle. You can prepare and refrigerate these cookie doughs one day and bake the cookies the next day.

Please review the basic rules in Cake Preparation and Cookie Preparation (pages 5 and 206) before making any of the cookies in this chapter.

FRAN'S BLACK WALNUT COOKIES

My friend Frances Nielsen of Oak Lawn, Illinois, makes these in big batches.

YIELD: THREE DOZEN COOKIES

3/4 cup sugar

1/2 cup brown sugar

1/2 cup (1 stick) margarine

1/4 cup egg whites or liquid egg substitute

1 teaspoon black walnut flavoring

2 cups all-purpose flour

1 teaspoon cream of tartar

1 teaspoon baking soda

1/4 teaspoon salt

1 cup chopped black walnuts

1/4 cup skim milk

Preheat oven to 375°F. Spray cookie sheets with cooking spray or line with aluminum foil. Set aside.

Using an electric mixer at medium speed, cream 1/2 cup sugar, brown sugar, and margarine together until light and fluffy. Add egg whites or liquid egg substitute and black walnut flavoring. Mix 1 minute at medium speed, scraping down the bowl before and after the addition.

Stir flour, cream of tartar, baking soda, salt, and nuts together to blend and add to the egg mixture. Mix at medium speed to blend.

Shape the dough into balls, using 1 tablespoon (a level No. 60 dipper) per ball. Dip the tops of the balls in milk, then in remaining 1/4 cup sugar, and place on the prepared cookie sheets. Bake for 10 to 12 minutes or until lightly browned and firm. Cool on wire racks.

VARIATION

FRAN'S ALMOND COOKIES: Substitute 1 teaspoon almond flavoring and 1 cup chopped almonds for the black walnut flavoring and black walnuts.

NUTRITIVE VALUES PER SERVING

Number of servings 36

---

calories 92 • carbohydrate 11 grams • protein 2 grams • fat 4 grams
sodium 71 milligrams • cholesterol 0 milligrams

Low-sodium diets: Omit salt
and use salt-free margarine.

ROLLED BUTTERMILK COOKIES

The nutritive values for these cookies are based on using a 2¹/₂-inch round cutter. To calculate nutritive values for a different-size cutter, multiply each of the values given by 24 for the values of the complete recipe. Then divide by the number of cookies produced using the different cutter. (This formula works with all cookie recipes.)

YIELD: TWO DOZEN COOKIES

¹/₂ cup (1 stick) margarine

1 cup sugar

¹/₄ cup egg whites or liquid egg
    substitute

1 teaspoon vanilla extract

3 cups all-purpose flour

¹/₂ teaspoon baking soda

¹/₄ teaspoon salt

2 tablespoons dry buttermilk

¹/₂ cup water, at room
    temperature

¹/₂ cup Vanilla Powdered Sugar
    Frosting (page 192)

Preheat oven to 375°F. Spray cookie sheets with cooking spray or line with aluminum foil. Set aside.

Using an electric mixer at medium speed, cream margarine and sugar together until light and fluffy. Add egg whites or liquid egg substitute and vanilla and mix at medium speed until creamy, scraping down the bowl before and after the addition.

Stir flour, baking soda, salt, and dry buttermilk together to blend and add, along with the water, to the creamy mixture. Mix well.

Roll the dough out ½ inch thick on a lightly floured surface. Cut cookies out with a 2½-inch round cutter and place on the prepared cookie sheets. Bake for 15 minutes or until the edges start to brown. Cool on wire racks. Then frost with Vanilla Powdered Sugar Frosting, using 1 teaspoon frosting per cookie.

NUTRITIVE VALUES PER SERVING

Number of servings 24

---

calories 147 • carbohydrate 24 grams • protein 2 grams • fat 4 grams
sodium 125 milligrams • cholesterol 0 milligrams

Low-sodium diets: Omit salt
and use salt-free margarine.

BUTTERSCOTCH CIRCLES

YIELD: THREE DOZEN COOKIES

3/4 cup (1 1/2 sticks) margarine

1 1/4 cups brown sugar

2 teaspoons caramel flavoring

1/4 cup egg whites or liquid egg substitute

3 1/4 cups all-purpose flour

1 teaspoon baking powder

1/2 teaspoon baking soda

1/4 teaspoon salt

1/2 cup chopped pecans

1/4 cup water, at room temperature

Preheat oven to 375°F. Spray cookie sheets with cooking spray or line with aluminum foil. Set aside.

Using an electric mixer at medium speed, cream margarine, brown sugar, and caramel flavoring together until light and fluffy. Add egg whites or liquid egg substitute and beat at medium speed until creamy, scraping down the bowl before and after the addition.

Stir flour, baking powder, baking soda, salt, and pecans together to blend and add, along with the water, to the creamy mixture. Mix at medium speed to blend.

Roll the dough out 1/3 inch thick on a lightly floured working surface. Cut cookies out with a 2 1/2-inch cutter and place on the prepared cookie sheets. Bake for 12 to 15 minutes or until firm. Cool on wire racks.

NUTRITIVE VALUES PER SERVING

Number of servings 36

calories 114 • carbohydrate 16 grams • protein 1 gram • fat 5 grams
sodium 101 milligrams • cholesterol 0 milligrams

Low-sodium diets: Omit salt.
Use salt-free margarine and low-sodium baking powder.

CHERRY KISSES

We shouldn't have egg yolks, but we can make the most of the egg whites. Meringues, like these Cherry Kisses, are one of my favorite ways to use them. The flavor of the kisses can be varied by changing the gelatin and adding a matching flavoring.

YIELD: TWO AND A HALF DOZEN COOKIES

Cornstarch, as needed

$\frac{1}{2}$ cup egg whites, at room temperature

$\frac{1}{4}$ teaspoon cream of tartar

$\frac{1}{4}$ teaspoon salt

1 3-ounce package cherry-flavored gelatin

$\frac{2}{3}$ cup sugar

1 teaspoon cherry flavoring (optional)

Preheat oven to 225°F. Line cookie sheets with aluminum foil and dust with cornstarch. Set aside.

Using an electric mixer with a whip attachment, beat egg whites, cream of tartar, and salt at high speed until foamy. Stir gelatin and sugar together to blend and, with the mixer running, add gradually to the egg whites. Continue to beat at high speed until stiff. Reduce mixer speed to low, add the cherry flavoring, and mix just to blend.

Drop the meringue with a large spoon onto the prepared cookie sheets, using 3 tablespoons meringue per kiss. Bake for 1 hour. Turn off the oven and let the meringue stay in the oven for another hour without opening the door.

Keep the kisses loosely covered in a cool, dry place or freeze in an airtight container up to 2 to 3 months.

NUTRITIVE VALUES PER SERVING

Number of servings 30

---

calories 28 • carbohydrate 7 grams • protein trace • fat 0 grams
sodium 24 milligrams • cholesterol 0 milligrams

Low-sodium diets: Omit salt.

CHOCOLATE CHERRY ROLLS

This is one of my favorite cookies. They are so pretty and I love the flavor. The variations are good too, but I really prefer the basic recipe.

YIELD: FOUR DOZEN COOKIES

CHOCOLATE DOUGH

1/2 cup (1 stick) margarine

1 cup sugar

1 teaspoon vanilla extract

1/4 cup egg whites or liquid egg substitute

1 1/2 cups all-purpose flour

3 tablespoons cocoa

1 teaspoon baking powder

1/4 teaspoon salt

1 teaspoon cherry flavoring

2 drops red food coloring

1/4 cup egg whites or liquid egg substitute

1 3/4 cups all-purpose flour

1 teaspoon baking powder

1/4 teaspoon salt

1/4 cup chopped maraschino cherries

CHERRY DOUGH

1/2 cup (1 stick) margarine

3/4 cup sugar

Prepare the chocolate dough: Using an electric mixer at medium speed, cream margarine, sugar, and vanilla until light and fluffy. Add egg whites or liquid egg substitute and mix at medium speed until creamy, scraping down the bowl before and after the addition. Stir flour, cocoa, baking powder, and salt together to blend and add to the egg mixture. Mix at medium speed until smooth. Place the chocolate dough in a bowl, cover, and chill from 1 hour to overnight.

Prepare the cherry dough: Using an electric mixer at medium speed, cream margarine, sugar, cherry flavoring, and food coloring together until light and fluffy. Add egg whites or liquid egg substitute and mix at medium speed until creamy, scraping down the bowl before and after the addition. Stir flour, baking powder, and salt together to blend and add to the egg mixture, along with the cherries. Mix at medium speed until blended. Place the cherry dough in a bowl, cover, and refrigerate from 2 hours to overnight.

When you are ready to make the rolls, roll the chocolate dough out on a lightly floured working surface to form a 16 by 9-inch rectangle. Roll the cherry dough out on lightly floured waxed paper to form another 16 by 9-inch rectangle. Brush away any excess flour with a pastry brush and roll the cherry dough loosely like a jelly roll. Unfold the roll of cherry dough onto the chocolate rectangle. Remove the waxed paper. Then roll up the doughs to form one 16-inch-long roll, with the chocolate dough on the outside and the cherry dough on the inside. Wrap the roll in waxed paper and refrigerate or freeze until firm.

Just before baking, unwrap the roll and cut into 48 equal slices, each about $1/3$ inch thick. Place on cookie sheets that have been sprayed with cooking spray or lined with aluminum foil and bake in a preheated 350°F oven for 12 to 15 minutes or until firm. Cool on wire racks.

VARIATIONS

1. CHOCOLATE PEPPERMINT ROLLS: Omit vanilla from chocolate dough and add 1 teaspoon peppermint flavoring. Omit cherry flavoring, red food coloring, and maraschino cherries from the cherry dough. Add 1 teaspoon vanilla and $1/3$ cup chopped nuts to the plain dough.

2. CHOCOLATE LEMON ROLLS: Omit cherry flavoring, red food coloring, and maraschino cherries from the cherry dough and add 1 teaspoon lemon extract, 1 tablespoon grated fresh or finely chopped dried lemon rind, and 1 or 2 drops yellow food coloring.

3. CHOCOLATE ALMOND ROLLS: Omit cherry flavoring, red food coloring, and maraschino cherries from the cherry dough. Add 1 teaspoon almond extract and ¹/₂ cup chopped almonds.

NUTRITIVE VALUES PER SERVING

Number of servings 48

---

calories 95 • carbohydrate 14 grams • protein 1 gram • fat 4 grams
sodium 85 milligrams • cholesterol 0 milligrams

Low-sodium diets: Omit salt.
Use salt-free margarine and low-sodium baking powder.

CHOCOLATE CRACKLE COOKIES

If you don't want to roll these cookies in sugar, you can just put them on the cookie sheets and bake them without, though they aren't as pretty and don't taste quite as good.

YIELD: THREE DOZEN COOKIES

¹/₂ cup (1 stick) margarine

1¹/₄ cups sugar

¹/₄ cup light corn syrup

¹/₄ cup egg whites

2 teaspoons vanilla extract

2 cups all-purpose flour

¹/₃ cup cocoa

1¹/₂ teaspoons baking soda

¹/₂ teaspoon salt

2 tablespoons water

Preheat oven to 350°F. Spray cookie sheets with cooking spray or line with aluminum foil. Set aside.

Using an electric mixer at medium speed, cream margarine, 1 cup sugar, and corn syrup together until light. Add egg whites and vanilla and mix at medium speed until creamy, scraping down the bowl before and after the addition.

Stir flour, cocoa, baking soda, and salt together to blend well and add to the creamy mixture, along with the water. Mix at medium speed to blend well.

Shape the dough into balls, using 1 tablespoon dough (a level No. 60 dipper) per ball. Roll the balls in the remaining ¼ cup sugar, if desired, and place on the prepared cookie sheets. Bake for 12 to 14 minutes or until firm. Cool on wire racks.

NUTRITIVE VALUES PER SERVING

Number of servings 36

---

calories 82 • carbohydrate 14 grams • protein 1 gram • fat 3 grams • sodium 98 milligrams • cholesterol 0 milligrams

---

Low-sodium diets: Omit salt
and use salt-free margarine.

CHOCOLATE CRISPS

These cookies are a favorite of my godchild, Vicki Glastetter, of Redlands, California. She says they make a wonderful snack when she is painting in her studio. The nutritive values are calculated for cookies made using a 2½-inch cutter.

FORMED COOKIES

1 cup (2 sticks) margarine

1³/₄ cups sugar

2 teaspoons vanilla extract

1 teaspoon chocolate flavoring (optional)

¹/₂ cup egg whites or liquid egg substitute

3 cups all-purpose flour

¹/₃ cup cocoa

2 teaspoons baking powder

¹/₄ teaspoon salt

Using an electric mixer at medium speed, cream margarine and sugar together until light and fluffy. Add flavorings and egg whites or liquid egg substitute and mix at medium speed until smooth, scraping down the bowl before and after the addition.

Stir flour, cocoa, baking powder, and salt together to blend and add to the egg mixture. Mix at medium speed to blend. Then cover and refrigerate from 2 hours to overnight.

Return the dough to room temperature and roll out ¹/₄ inch thick on a lightly floured working surface. Cut cookies out using a 2¹/₂-inch round cutter. Place on cookie sheets that have been sprayed with cooking spray or lined with aluminum foil. Bake in a preheated 350°F oven for 8 to 10 minutes or until almost firm. Do not overbake. Cool on wire racks. Store in a loosely covered container or freeze up to 3 months.

VARIATIONS

1. CHOCOLATE PEPPERMINT CRISPS: Add 1 teaspoon peppermint flavoring along with the vanilla.

2. CHOCOLATE WALNUT CRISPS: Omit vanilla and add 1 teaspoon black walnut flavoring and ³/₄ cup finely chopped walnuts, preferably black, along with the flour mixture.

3. CHOCOLATE RAISIN CRISPS: Add ¾ cup chopped raisins along with the flour mixture.

NUTRITIVE VALUES PER SERVING

Number of servings 48

---

calories 93 • carbohydrate 14 grams • protein 1 gram • fat 4 grams
sodium 73 milligrams • cholesterol 0 milligrams

Low-sodium diets: Omit salt.
Use salt-free margarine and low-sodium baking powder.

DATE PINWHEEL COOKIES

YIELD: TWO DOZEN COOKIES

8 ounces (1½ cups) chopped pitted dates

¼ plus ⅓ cup sugar

¼ cup water

½ cup (1 stick) margarine

⅓ cup brown sugar

½ cup egg whites or liquid egg substitute

1 teaspoon vanilla extract

2¼ cups all-purpose flour

½ teaspoon baking soda

¼ teaspoon salt

Place dates, ¼ cup sugar, and water in a small saucepan and cook over medium heat, stirring, until thickened. Cool to room temperature.

Using an electric mixer at medium speed, cream margarine, remaining ⅓ cup sugar, and brown sugar together until light and fluffy. Add egg whites or liquid egg substitute and vanilla and mix at medium speed until creamy, scraping down the bowl before and after the addition.

Stir flour, baking soda, and salt together to blend well and add to the creamy mixture. Mix at medium speed to blend. Then cover and refrigerate for 1 to 3 hours.

Roll the dough out into a rectangle about ½ inch thick on a lightly floured surface. Spread evenly with the date mixture and then roll up like a jelly roll. The roll should be a little over 6 inches long. Wrap in waxed paper and refrigerate again for 1 to 3 hours.

Just before baking, unwrap the dough and slice into 24 equal slices each about ¼ inch thick. Place on cookie sheets that have been sprayed with cooking spray or lined with aluminum foil. Bake in a preheated 350°F oven for 12 minutes or until lightly browned. Cool on wire racks.

NUTRITIVE VALUES PER SERVING

Number of servings 24

---

calories 128 • carbohydrate 22 grams • protein 2 grams • fat 4 grams
• sodium 93 milligrams • cholesterol 0 milligrams

Low-sodium diets: Omit salt
and use salt-free margarine.

MARGARINE COOKIES

These cookies, which are my version of the ever-popular butter cookies, can be decorated or formed in many different shapes for holidays and special occasions. They freeze well and will keep for several weeks if stored in an airtight container at room temperature.

YIELD: FIVE DOZEN COOKIES

$^1/_2$ cup (1 stick) margarine, softened

$1^1/_4$ cups powdered or confectioners' sugar

2 large egg whites

2 teaspoons vanilla extract

1 teaspoon butter flavoring (optional)

2 drops yellow food coloring (optional)

3 cups cake flour

$1^1/_2$ teaspoons cream of tartar

1 teaspoon baking soda

$^1/_4$ teaspoon salt

Spray cookie sheets with cooking spray or line with aluminum foil. Set aside.

Using an electric mixer at medium speed, cream margarine and powdered sugar together until light and fluffy. Add egg whites, flavorings, and food coloring and beat for 1 minute at medium speed, scraping down the bowl before and after the addition.

Stir flour, cream of tartar, baking soda, and salt together to blend. Add to the egg mixture and mix at low speed until smooth.

Transfer the dough to a pastry bag or cookie press and press cookies out onto the prepared cookie sheets, using about 2 teaspoons of dough for each cookie. Refrigerate for 30 minutes. Then bake in a preheated 375°F oven for 8 to 10 minutes or until lightly browned. Cool on wire racks.

NUTRITIVE VALUES PER SERVING

Number of servings 60

---

calories 53 • carbohydrate 6 grams • protein 1 gram • fat 3 grams
• sodium 60 milligrams • cholesterol 0 milligrams

Low-sodium diets: Omit salt
and use salt-free margarine.

MOLASSES COOKIES

This dough makes excellent gingerbread boys or girls, and the whole house smells good when they are baking.

YIELD: TWO AND A HALF DOZEN COOKIES

¹/₂ **cup (1 stick) margarine**	1¹/₂ **teaspoons baking soda**
¹/₂ **cup sugar**	¹/₂ **teaspoon ground ginger**
¹/₂ **cup molasses**	¹/₂ **teaspoon cinnamon**
3 **cups all-purpose flour**	¹/₂ **cup boiling water**

Preheat oven to 350°F. Spray cookie sheets with cooking spray or line with aluminum foil. Set aside.

Using an electric mixer at medium speed, beat margarine, sugar, and molasses together until smooth and creamy. Stir flour, baking soda, ginger, and cinnamon together to blend and add, along with the boiling water, to the creamy mixture. Mix at medium speed until blended.

Roll the dough out ¹/₃ inch thick on a lightly floured surface. Cut cookies out using a 2¹/₂-inch round cutter. Place on the prepared cookie sheets and bake for 10 to 12 minutes or until browned on the bottoms. Cool on wire racks.

NUTRITIVE VALUES PER SERVING

Number of servings 30

---

calories 92 • carbohydrate 15 grams • protein 1 gram • fat 3 grams
sodium 89 milligrams • cholesterol 0 milligrams

Low-sodium diets: Use salt-free margarine.

RIBBON COOKIES

These cookies are pretty and not complicated to prepare. Sometimes I vary the coloring and use different kinds of nuts or candied fruit for the different layers.

YIELD: FOUR DOZEN COOKIES

1 cup (2 sticks) margarine

3/4 cup sugar

3/4 cup brown sugar

3/4 cup egg whites or liquid egg substitute

2 teaspoons vanilla extract

4 cups all-purpose flour

1 teaspoon baking soda

1/4 teaspoon salt

1 drop red food coloring

1/4 cup chopped candied red cherries

1 drop green food coloring

1/3 cup chopped Brazil nuts

2 tablespoons poppyseeds

Using an electric mixer at medium speed, cream margarine and sugars together until light and fluffy. Add egg whites or liquid egg substitute and vanilla and mix at medium speed for 30 seconds, scraping down the bowl before and after the addition.

Stir flour, baking soda, and salt together to blend and add to the egg mixture. Mix at medium speed until smooth.

Turn the dough out onto a lightly floured working surface and divide into three equal portions. Add red food coloring and candied cherries to one portion of dough. Add green food coloring and Brazil nuts to the second portion and the poppyseeds to the third portion. Line a 9 by 5 by 3-inch loaf pan with waxed paper, grease the waxed paper with margarine, and press the cherry layer evenly in the pan. Add the poppyseed layer next and top with the nut layer, making sure to press each layer into the pan evenly. Cover with waxed paper or aluminum foil and freeze or refrigerate until firm.

Just before baking, remove the dough from the pan, remove the waxed paper, and cut the dough lengthwise through the center into two equal portions. Cut each half of the dough into 24 equal slices, each about $1/3$ inch thick. Place the slices on cookie sheets that have been sprayed with cooking spray or lined with aluminum foil. Bake in a preheated 350°F oven for 10 minutes or until firm and lightly browned. Cool on wire racks.

NUTRITIVE VALUES PER SERVING

Number of servings 48

calories 106 • carbohydrate 16 grams • protein 2 grams • fat 4 grams
sodium 81 milligrams • cholesterol 0 milligrams

Low-sodium diets: Omit salt
and use salt-free margarine.

SPOON RIVER COOKIES

This recipe, adapted for a low-cholesterol, low-fat, low-sugar diet, is based on a cookie that was popular at a bakery in London Mills, Illinois. That town is located in the Spoon River area made famous by Edgar Lee Masters in his Spoon River Anthology. *These cookies, which reached the height of their fame around the time of the First World War, were generally served with coffee.*

COOKIES

YIELD: TWO DOZEN COOKIES

½ cup (1 stick) margarine

1 cup sugar

¼ cup egg whites or liquid egg substitute

1 teaspoon vanilla extract

1 teaspoon lemon extract

2 cups all-purpose flour

½ teaspoon nutmeg (optional)

½ teaspoon baking powder

½ teaspoon baking soda

⅛ teaspoon salt

1 tablespoon dry buttermilk

Using an electric mixer at medium speed, cream margarine and sugar together until light and fluffy. Add egg whites or liquid egg substitute and flavorings and mix at medium speed until creamy, scraping down the bowl before and after the addition.

Stir flour, nutmeg, baking powder, baking soda, salt, and dry buttermilk together to blend and add to the egg mixture. Mix at medium speed until smooth. Then cover and refrigerate from 3 hours to overnight.

Return dough almost to room temperature and roll out ¼ inch thick on a floured working surface. Cut out cookies using a 2½-inch round cutter or the equivalent fancy cutter. Place the cookies on cookie sheets that have been sprayed with cooking spray or lined with aluminum foil. Bake in a preheated 350°F oven for 10 minutes or until lightly browned. Cool on wire racks.

NUTRITIVE VALUES PER SERVING

Number of servings 24

calories 107 • carbohydrate 17 grams • protein 2 grams • fat 4 grams
sodium 92 milligrams • cholesterol 0 milligrams

Low-sodium diets: Omit salt.
Use salt-free margarine and low-sodium baking powder.

BARS

APPLESAUCE BROWNIES

BUTTERSCOTCH BROWNIES

FUDGE BROWNIES

LIGHT CHOCOLATE BROWNIES

APRICOT DATE BARS

CHOCOLATE APPLESAUCE BARS

BANANA BRAN BARS

DATE BARS

GREAT OATMEAL BARS

FROSTED OATMEAL BARS

HARVEST OATMEAL BARS

DATE OATMEAL BARS

OATEN BARS

PIONEER BARS

PUMPKIN PECAN BARS

PUFFED WHEAT BARS

BARS ARE a cross between cakes and cookies. Some have the consistency of a cake and others are crisp like a cookie. Like all cookies, the texture of a bar depends upon the proportion of flour, fat, and sugar. A bar with a higher proportion of flour will be soft, and a bar with a higher proportion of fat and sugar will be crisp. Since we are trying to reduce the fat and sugar content of our bars, most of the bars in this chapter are soft. The texture of a bar also depends upon the amount of batter in the pan. If it is too thin, the bars will be hard and dry. With too much batter, the bars will be soft and cakelike.

Most drop cookie recipes will make good bars. This is helpful when there isn't enough time to make individual cookies. If the recipe calls for pushing the cookies down with the back of a spoon before they are baked, they will probably require the addition of up to $^1/_4$ cup water in order to achieve the proper spreading consistency. However, most of the drop cookie recipes in this book can be spread after the basic recipe has been prepared. A recipe for 2 dozen average-size cookies will make an 11 by 15-inch jelly roll pan of bars (24 servings), and a recipe for 3 dozen average-size cookies will make a 12 by 18-inch half sheet pan of bars (36 servings).

To bake a cookie recipe as bars, spread the dough evenly in a pan that has been sprayed with cooking spray or greased with margarine and bake at 350° or 375°F (depending on the original recipe) for 20 to 30 minutes or until the bars pull away from the sides of the pan and a cake tester inserted in the center comes out clean. Bars that are based on cookie recipes should be cooled slightly in the pan and cut while they are still warm. The yield should remain the same so nutritive values are not changed.

Bars can be cut, covered with an airtight cover or aluminum foil, and refrigerated or frozen until they are needed. I usually take them out of the pan after they are cut and freeze them in a freezer bag for later use. I like to make several pans of bars at a time and freeze an assortment of them in each freezer bag so I can have a variety of bars to serve without having to fish around in many different bags.

Please review the basic rules in Cake Preparation and Cookie Preparation (pages 5 and 206) before making any of the bars in this chapter.

APPLESAUCE BROWNIES

YIELD: TWO DOZEN BROWNIES

½ cup (1 stick) margarine

1 cup sugar

½ cup egg whites or liquid egg substitute

1 teaspoon vanilla extract

2 cups all-purpose flour

2 tablespoons cocoa

1 teaspoon baking soda

½ teaspoon salt

½ teaspoon cinnamon

2 cups unsweetened applesauce

½ cup raisins

½ cup chopped black or English walnuts

Preheat oven to 350°F. Grease a 9 by 13-inch cake pan with margarine or cooking spray and set aside.

Using an electric mixer at medium speed, cream margarine and sugar together until light and fluffy. Add egg whites or liquid egg substitute and vanilla and mix at medium speed for 30 seconds, scraping down the bowl before and after the addition.

Stir flour, cocoa, baking soda, salt, and cinnamon together to blend and add to the egg mixture, along with the applesauce, raisins, and nuts. Mix at medium speed until creamy.

Spread the batter evenly in the prepared pan. Bake for 30 minutes or until lightly browned and a cake tester inserted in the center comes out clean. Cool to room temperature. Frost if desired.

NUTRITIVE VALUES PER SERVING

Number of servings 24

---

calories 140 • carbohydrate 22 grams • protein 2 grams • fat 5 grams
sodium 132 milligrams • cholesterol 0 milligrams

Low-sodium diets: Omit salt
and use salt-free margarine.

BUTTERSCOTCH BROWNIES

YIELD: TWO DOZEN BROWNIES

1½ cups brown sugar

¾ cup (1½ sticks) margarine

½ cup egg whites or liquid egg substitute

1 teaspoon caramel flavoring

2½ cups all-purpose flour

1½ teaspoons baking powder

½ teaspoon salt

⅓ cup water, at room temperature

½ cup chopped pecans

Preheat oven to 350°F. Grease an 11 by 15-inch jelly roll pan with margarine or cooking spray and set aside.

Using an electric mixer at medium speed, cream brown sugar and margarine together until light and fluffy. Add egg whites or liquid egg substitute and caramel flavoring and mix at medium speed until creamy, scraping down the bowl before and after the addition.

Stir flour, baking powder, and salt together and add to the creamy mixture, along with the water and pecans. Mix at medium speed until creamy.

Spread the batter evenly in the prepared pan. Bake for 25 to 30 minutes or until the bars are lightly browned and pull away from the sides of the pan. Cool in the pan on a wire rack. Cut while still warm.

NUTRITIVE VALUES PER SERVING

Number of servings 24

---

calories 166 • carbohydrate 24 grams • protein 2 grams • fat 7 grams
sodium 146 milligrams • cholesterol 0 milligrams

Low-sodium diets: Omit salt.
Use salt-free margarine and low-sodium baking powder.

FUDGE BROWNIES

These dark, rich brownies taste as though they were made with melted chocolate and butter, when actually they are made with cocoa and margarine. They aren't low in calories but they are cholesterol-free and absolutely luscious.

YIELD: 16 BROWNIES

1 cup sugar

1¼ cups all-purpose flour

⅓ cup cocoa

½ teaspoon baking powder

½ cup (1 stick) margarine, softened

¼ cup egg whites or liquid egg substitute

¼ cup light corn syrup

1 teaspoon vanilla extract

¼ cup chopped black or English walnuts

Preheat oven to 350°F. Grease a 9-inch square cake pan with margarine or cooking spray and set aside.

Place sugar, flour, cocoa, and baking powder in the bowl of an electric mixer and mix at low speed for 30 seconds to blend. Add margarine, egg whites or liquid egg substitute, corn syrup, vanilla, and nuts and mix at medium speed to blend.

Spread the batter evenly in the prepared pan. Bake for 20 to 25 minutes or until the brownies pull away from the sides of the pan and are almost firm in the center. Cool in the pan on a wire rack. Cut while still warm.

NUTRITIVE VALUES PER SERVING

Number of servings 16

---

calories 160 • carbohydrate 25 grams • protein 3 grams • fat 7 grams
sodium 103 milligrams • cholesterol 0 milligrams

Low-sodium diets: Use salt-free margarine
and low-sodium baking powder.

LIGHT CHOCOLATE BROWNIES

Brownies are so popular that I thought it might be a good idea to include more than one recipe. See page 269 for Fudge Brownies, another of my favorites.

YIELD: THREE DOZEN BROWNIES

3/4 cup (1 1/2 sticks) margarine

3/4 cup sugar

3/4 cup brown sugar

1/2 cup egg whites or liquid egg substitute

1 teaspoon vanilla extract

2 1/4 cups all-purpose flour

1/4 cup cocoa

1 teaspoon baking soda

1/2 teaspoon salt

1 cup chopped black or English walnuts

Preheat oven to 350°F. Grease an 11 by 15-inch jelly roll pan with margarine or cooking spray and set aside.

Using an electric mixer at medium speed, cream margarine and sugars together until light and fluffy. Add egg whites or liquid egg substitute and vanilla and mix at medium speed until creamy, scraping down the bowl before and after the addition.

Stir flour, cocoa, baking soda, salt, and nuts together to blend and add to the creamy mixture. Mix at medium speed to blend.

Spread the batter in the prepared pan. Bake for 20 to 25 minutes or until the brownies pull away from the sides of the pan and are almost firm in the center. Cool in the pan on a wire rack. Cut while still warm.

NUTRITIVE VALUES PER SERVING

Number of servings 36

---

calories 113 • carbohydrate 16 grams • protein 2 grams • fat 5 grams
sodium 120 milligrams • cholesterol 0 milligrams

Low-sodium diets: Omit salt
and use salt-free margarine.

APRICOT DATE BARS

YIELD: 32 BARS

³/₄ cup (1¹/₂ sticks) margarine

1¹/₂ cups sugar

¹/₂ cup egg whites or liquid egg
  substitute

2 teaspoons vanilla extract

3 cups all-purpose flour

1 teaspoon baking soda

¹/₂ teaspoon salt

¹/₄ cup water, at room
  temperature

¹/₂ cup chopped dates

¹/₂ cup chopped dried apricots

Preheat oven to 375°F. Grease an 11 by 15-inch jelly roll pan with margarine or cooking spray and set aside.

Using an electric mixer at medium speed, cream margarine and sugar together until light and fluffy. Add egg whites or liquid egg substitute and vanilla and beat at medium speed until creamy, scraping down the bowl before and after the addition.

Stir flour, baking soda, and salt together and add to the creamy mixture, along with the water. Beat at medium speed until creamy. Stir in the dates and apricots and spread evenly in the prepared pan. Bake for 25 minutes or until the bars are lightly browned and pull away from the sides of the pan. Cool in the pan on a wire rack. Cut while still warm.

NUTRITIVE VALUES PER SERVING

Number of servings 32

---

calories 131 • carbohydrate 22 grams • protein 2 grams • fat 4 grams
sodium 116 milligrams • cholesterol 0 milligrams

Low-sodium diets: Omit salt
and use salt-free margarine.

CHOCOLATE APPLESAUCE BARS

YIELD: TWO DOZEN BARS

2 cups all-purpose flour

1 cup sugar

$1/4$ cup cocoa

1 teaspoon baking soda

1 teaspoon apple pie spice or cinnamon

$1/2$ teaspoon salt

$1/4$ cup chopped English walnuts

$1/4$ cup raisins

$1^1/2$ cups unsweetened applesauce

$1/2$ cup vegetable oil

1 teaspoon lemon juice

1 teaspoon vanilla extract

Preheat oven to 375°F. Grease an 11 by 15-inch jelly roll pan with margarine or cooking spray and set aside.

Place flour, sugar, cocoa, baking soda, apple pie spice or cinnamon, salt, nuts, and raisins in the bowl of an electric mixer and mix at low speed for

30 seconds to blend. Beat applesauce, oil, lemon juice, and vanilla together with a fork to blend and add to the flour mixture. Beat at medium speed for 1 minute, scraping down the bowl once during the mixing.

Spread the batter evenly in the prepared pan. Bake for 20 to 25 minutes or until a cake tester inserted in the center comes out clean. Cool on a wire rack. Frost if desired.

NUTRITIVE VALUES PER SERVING

Number of servings 24

---

calories 132 • carbohydrate 20 grams • protein 1 gram • fat 6 grams
sodium 80 milligrams • cholesterol 0 milligrams

Low-sodium diets: Omit salt.

BANANA BRAN BARS

YIELD: 28 BARS

½ cup (1 stick) margarine

1 cup sugar

¼ cup egg whites or liquid egg substitute

½ teaspoon banana flavoring or vanilla extract

½ teaspoon black walnut flavoring

2 medium bananas, sliced ½ inch thick

2 cups all-purpose flour

1 teaspoon baking powder

½ teaspoon salt

1 cup Bran Buds, All Bran, 100% Bran, or Fiber One cereal

½ cup chopped black or English walnuts

1 cup powdered or confectioners' sugar

2 tablespoons water

Preheat oven to 375°F. Grease an 11 by 15-inch jelly roll pan with margarine or cooking spray and set aside.

Using an electric mixer at medium speed, cream margarine and sugar together until light and fluffy. Add egg whites or liquid egg substitute and flavorings and mix at medium speed until creamy, scraping down the bowl before and after the addition. Add bananas and mix at medium speed until creamy.

Stir flour, baking powder, salt, cereal, and nuts together to mix and add to the banana mixture. Mix at medium speed only until all of the flour is absorbed.

Spread the batter evenly in the prepared pan. Bake for 25 to 30 minutes or until lightly browned and a cake tester inserted in the center comes out clean.

While the bars are baking, combine the powdered sugar and water and stir until smooth to form a glaze. Spread the glaze evenly over the hot bars. Cool on a wire rack to room temperature and cut.

NUTRITIVE VALUES PER SERVING

Number of servings 28

---

calories 128 • carbohydrate 22 grams • protein 2 grams • fat 3 grams
sodium 108 milligrams • cholesterol 0 milligrams

Low-sodium diets: Omit salt.
Use salt-free margarine and low-sodium baking powder.

DATE BARS

YIELD: TWO DOZEN BARS

½ cup (1 stick) margarine

½ cup sugar

½ cup brown sugar

½ cup egg whites or liquid egg substitute

1 teaspoon vanilla extract

2½ cups all-purpose flour

1 teaspoon baking soda

½ teaspoon salt

1 cup chopped pitted dates

Preheat oven to 375°F. Grease an 11 by 15-inch jelly roll pan with margarine or cooking spray and set aside.

Using an electric mixer at medium speed, cream margarine and sugars together until light and fluffy. Add egg whites or liquid egg substitute and vanilla and beat at medium speed for 1 minute, scraping down the bowl before and after the addition.

Stir flour, baking soda, and salt together to blend well and add, along with the dates, to the egg mixture. Mix at medium speed until creamy.

Spread the batter evenly in the prepared pan. Bake for 20 minutes or until browned and firm. Cool on a wire rack.

NUTRITIVE VALUES PER SERVING

Number of servings 24

---

calories 137 • carbohydrate 24 grams • protein 2 grams • fat 4 grams
sodium 134 milligrams • cholesterol 0 milligrams

Low-sodium diets: Omit salt
and use salt-free margarine.

GREAT OATMEAL BARS

These bars are a truly wonderful oatmeal treat. The recipe came from Vivian Lott of Volga, Iowa, who tells me she frequently leaves out the pecans and makes Frosted Oatmeal Bars (page 279).

YIELD: THREE DOZEN BARS

³/₄ cup (1¹/₂ sticks) margarine

³/₄ cup sugar

³/₄ cup brown sugar

¹/₃ cup egg whites or liquid egg substitute

1 teaspoon vanilla extract

1¹/₂ cups all-purpose flour

1 teaspoon baking soda

3 cups rolled oats

1 cup chopped pecans

Preheat oven to 350°F. Grease an 11 by 15-inch jelly roll pan with margarine or cooking spray and set aside.

Using an electric mixer at medium speed, cream margarine and sugars together until light and fluffy. Add egg whites or liquid egg substitute and vanilla and mix at medium speed until creamy, scraping down the bowl before and after the addition.

Stir flour, baking soda, and oatmeal together and add to the creamy mixture. Mix at medium speed until creamy. Then stir in the pecans.

Spread the batter evenly in the prepared pan. Bake for 20 to 25 minutes or until the bars are lightly browned and pull away from the sides of the pan. Cool on a wire rack.

VARIATIONS

1. FROSTED OATMEAL BARS: Omit pecans and frost with Orange Powdered Sugar Frosting (page 193) or Lemon Powdered Sugar Frosting (page 192).

2. HARVEST OATMEAL BARS: Omit pecans and add 1 teaspoon cinnamon and 1 cup raisins.

3. DATE OATMEAL BARS: Reduce pecans to ½ cup and add ½ cup chopped dates.

NUTRITIVE VALUES PER SERVING
Number of servings 36

calories 133 • carbohydrate 18 grams • protein 2 grams • fat 6 grams
sodium 73 milligrams • cholesterol 0 milligrams

Low-sodium diets: Use salt-free margarine.

OATEN BARS

YIELD: TWO DOZEN BARS

½ cup vegetable oil

½ cup brown sugar

¼ cup sugar

¼ cup egg whites or liquid egg substitute

2 teaspoons vanilla extract

1 cup all-purpose flour

1 cup oat bran cereal

1 cup rolled oats

1 teaspoon baking powder

1 teaspoon baking soda

½ teaspoon salt

1 teaspoon cinnamon

½ cup raisins

¼ cup chopped pecans

½ cup water, at room temperature

Preheat oven to 350°F. Grease an 11 by 15-inch jelly roll pan with margarine or cooking spray and set aside.

Place oil, sugars, egg whites or liquid egg substitute, and vanilla in the bowl of an electric mixer and mix at medium speed for 1 minute.

Stir flour, bran cereal, oatmeal, baking powder, baking soda, salt, and cinnamon together and add to the egg mixture along with the raisins, pecans, and water. Mix at medium speed until well blended.

Spread the batter evenly in the prepared pan. Bake for 20 to 25 minutes or until the bars are lightly browned and pull away from the sides of the pan. Cool on a wire rack.

NUTRITIVE VALUES PER SERVING

Number of servings 24

---

calories 128 • carbohydrate 18 grams • protein 2 grams • fat 6 grams
sodium 99 milligrams • cholesterol 0 milligrams

Low-sodium diets: Omit salt
and use low-sodium baking powder.

PIONEER BARS

These bars include ingredients that were plentiful here in Iowa around the turn of the century. There were very few spices available to local cooks during that time, but they made the best of what they had and developed some very fine recipes.

YIELD: 32 BARS

1½ cups water, plus additional
    as needed

½ cup (1 stick) margarine

1 cup sugar

1 cup raisins

1½ teaspoons cinnamon

¼ teaspoon allspice

3 cups all-purpose flour

1½ teaspoons baking soda

½ teaspoon salt

½ cup egg whites

1 cup powdered or
    confectioners' sugar

1 teaspoon lemon extract

Preheat oven to 350°F. Grease an 11 by 15-inch jelly roll pan with margarine or cooking spray and set aside.

Place 1½ cups water, margarine, sugar, raisins, cinnamon, and allspice in a small saucepan and bring to a boil, stirring to dissolve the sugar. Remove from heat, cover, and cool to room temperature.

Place flour, baking soda, and salt in the bowl of an electric mixer and mix at low speed to blend well.

Stir egg whites into the cooled raisin mixture and add to the flour mixture. Mix at medium speed only until creamy.

Spread the batter evenly in the prepared pan. Bake for 30 minutes or until lightly browned and firm in the center. Cool on a wire rack.

Combine powdered sugar, lemon extract, and enough water to make a thin frosting. Drizzle over the cooled bars.

NUTRITIVE VALUES PER SERVING

Number of servings 32

---

calories 115 • carbohydrate 21 grams • protein 2 grams • fat 3 grams
sodium 112 milligrams • cholesterol 0 milligrams

Low-sodium diets: Omit salt
and use salt-free margarine.

PUMPKIN PECAN BARS

YIELD: 28 BARS

1 cup egg whites or liquid egg substitute, at room temperature

²/₃ cup vegetable oil

1¹/₂ cups brown sugar

2 cups canned pumpkin puree

1 teaspoon vanilla extract

2 cups all-purpose flour

2 teaspoons baking powder

³/₄ teaspoon baking soda

¹/₂ teaspoon salt

1¹/₂ teaspoons pumpkin pie spice

¹/₂ cup chopped pecans

Preheat oven to 350°F. Grease an 11 by 15-inch jelly roll pan with margarine or cooking spray and set aside.

Place egg whites or liquid egg substitute, oil, brown sugar, pumpkin, and vanilla in the bowl of an electric mixer and mix at medium speed until smooth.

Stir flour, baking powder, baking soda, salt, pumpkin pie spice, and pecans together to blend and add to the pumpkin mixture. Mix at medium speed until smooth.

Spread the batter evenly in the prepared pan. Bake for 25 minutes or until lightly browned and a cake tester inserted in the center comes out clean. Cool on a wire rack. Frost if desired.

NUTRITIVE VALUES PER SERVING

Number of servings 28

---

calories 145 • carbohydrate 20 grams • protein 2 grams • fat 7 grams
sodium 104 milligrams • cholesterol 0 milligrams

Low-sodium diets: Omit salt
and use low-sodium baking powder.

PUFFED WHEAT BARS

It is important to work quickly when making these sticky bars. If you dip your hands in cold water when you press down the mixture, you'll find it is much easier to manage.

YIELD: TWO DOZEN BARS

2 tablespoons margarine

½ cup chunky peanut butter

1 teaspoon vanilla extract

1 10-ounce package
marshmallows

½ cup powdered or
confectioners' sugar

6 cups puffed wheat cereal

Place margarine and peanut butter in a large microwave-safe bowl or pitcher and microwave on high power until margarine is melted. Add vanilla and stir until smooth. Add marshmallows and return to the microwave. Microwave on high power until the marshmallows are puffy and very soft. Add powdered sugar and mix to blend.

Pour the marshmallow mixture over the puffed wheat cereal and mix thoroughly.

Press the mixture evenly in an 11 by 15-inch jelly roll pan that has been greased with margarine or cooking spray. Let stand at room temperature until firm before cutting.

NUTRITIVE VALUES PER SERVING

Number of servings 24

---

calories 98 • carbohydrate 15 grams • protein trace • fat 3 grams
sodium 45 milligrams • cholesterol 0 milligrams

Low-sodium diets: Use salt-free margarine
and low-sodium peanut butter, if available.

INDEX